NARRATIVE
ANALYSIS

CATHERINE KOHLER RIESSMAN
Boston University

Qualitative Research Methods
Volume 30

SAGE PUBLICATIONS
International Educational and Professional Publisher
Newbury Park   London   New Delhi

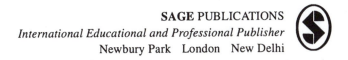

To Elliot

For information address:

SAGE Publications, Inc.
2455 Teller Road
Newbury Park, California 91320
E-mail: order@sagepub.com

SAGE Publications Ltd.
6 Bonhill Street
London EC2A 4PU
United Kingdom

SAGE Publications India Pvt. Ltd.
M-32 Market
Greater Kailash I
New Delhi 110 048 India

Printed in the United States of America

Library of Congress Cataloging-in-Publication Data

Riessman, Catherine Kohler, 1939-
    Narrative analysis / Catherine Kohler Riessman.
        p.   cm.   — (Qualitative research methods ; v. 30)
    Includes bibliographical references.
    ISBN 978-0-8039-4753-5 (cl.) — ISBN 978-0-8039-4754-2 (pb)
    1. Discourse analysis, Narrative.   I. Title.   II. Series.
P302.7.R54   1993
302.2—dc20   93-25555

08 16 15

Sage Production Editor: Judith L. Hunter

CONTENTS

EDITORS' INTRODUCTION

Catherine Kohler Riessman, in this 30th volume of the Sage Qualitative Research Methods Series, has made the method of narrative analysis more systematic and useful for fieldworkers. Building on past approaches, she introduces and illustrates forms of narrative analysis of women's lives and health concerns. Although much has been written about narrative and its role in the study of lives, nothing has been written about the logic of narrative analysis—how to carry it out and why.

The author locates herself and her work first in a personal narrative, then illustrates three types of narrative analysis, pointing out their relative strengths and weaknesses. In the third section of the book, she shows how she carries out narrative work, from telling to transcribing to analyzing. Her detailed and clear approach results in an excellent paradigm for others who are struggling with texts rather than wedded to technique.

This book is also embedded in Riessman's analyses of divorce narratives and women's situations and health concerns. It is thus a contribution to method and to the substantive study of women's lives and well-being.

—Peter K. Manning
John Van Maanen
Marc L. Miller

PREFACE: LOCATING MYSELF

The construction of any work always bears the mark of the person who created it. So, before formally discussing narrative analysis, I begin by locating myself and the contexts that shaped the volume and authorize its point of view.

Students and colleagues in sociology, psychology, and social work pressed me to write this book. They came to my office, metaphorically drowning in a sea of interview transcripts, asking for *a* source, *a* reference. I remember a visit from a senior clinical psychology professor. She had just begun a study of resilience in women who had been sexually abused as children: The first interview had lasted 10 hours and resulted in a 300-page transcription. The informant had told many stories about important moments in her life, which my colleague recognized as narrative from clinical experience and reading. But her extensive training in mainstream research methods ill-prepared her for working with the kinds of texts she was generating. She asked for a methodological resource. I directed her to various examples of narrative work by sociolinguists and others, often in journals and edited collections that fell outside the established social science research tradition. Although talk was the object for study, the qualitative methods literature was largely silent about ways to approach long stretches of talk that took the form of narrative accounts.

My doctoral students, too, stimulated this book. In a memorable seminar on Qualitative Analysis of Clinical Data in 1992, we explored the narrative literature together and they used the concepts to creatively analyze stretches of talk they collected in research interviews—about becoming a mother, having breast cancer, experiencing race. Many of the emergent ideas from our discussions form the basis of this book.

My appreciation of the power of narrative goes back many years to when I was studying literature at Bard College in the late 1950s and extraordinary teachers pushed me to go beyond "loving" a book to examining how it was constructed. I remember a tutorial with Dwight Macdonald (having no idea at the time of his significance in literary criticism). We examined how Joyce's *Ulysses* was put together. Years later, in my otherwise excellent graduate training in medical sociology at Columbia University, interpretation of texts had seemingly little relevance, sadly, although a possible outcome was an intense interest in method. Mostly, narrative and sociology remained very far apart for me until years later.

Without the words to say it—a language for a method—I did not attend to storytelling. Working as a clinical social worker in the late 1960s, I had listened to and helped individuals make difficult events meaningful by putting them into an interpretive sequence, but I never dreamed that therapeutic conversations could be research materials and systematically investigated. In a consciousness-raising group during the early days of the recent feminist movement, many of us came to see our common oppression as women by narrating our personal experiences one by one as we went around the room. Few of us at the time ever thought these accounts could be data, texts about lives that could be interpreted to reveal intersections of the social, cultural, personal, and political.

Narrative and sociology got connected for me in the 1980s during a research project on gender and divorce (Riessman, 1990a), which I conducted with Naomi Gerstel. In structured interviews, women and men seized every opportunity in the conversation to tell about their experiences. Some developed long accounts of what had happened in their marriages to justify their divorces. I did not realize these were narratives until I struggled to code them. Applying traditional qualitative methods, I searched the texts for common thematic elements. But some individuals knitted together several themes into long accounts that had coherence and sequence, defying easy categorization. I found myself not wanting to fragment the long accounts into distinct thematic categories. There seemed to be a common structure beneath talk about a variety of topics. While I coded one interview, a respondent provided language for my trouble. As I have thought about it since, it was a "click moment" in my biography as a narrative researcher (Fonow & Cook, 1991).

Asked to state "in his own words the main causes of his separation," the man laughed and said "Well, you known, that's a real long story, but maybe I can sum it up by saying . . . ." I saw how others tried to tell long stories about their experiences in marriage and after, despite my best efforts to be a good social scientist, standardize interview procedures, elicit data that were comparable, and code them into a common set of thematic categories. Individuals recapitulated and reinterpreted their lives through story telling.

In a postdoctoral fellowship, Elliot Mishler was an invaluable teacher, guiding me to think about interviews as narrative. Not unlike students who consult me now, I came to the Laboratory in Social Psychiatry at

Harvard Medical School in 1984 (thanks to an award from NIMH, grant #5F32MH09206) drowning in transcripts. He sent me to resources in narrative theory, sociolinguistics, and interpretive social science. He rekindled an interest, dormant since my Bard College days, in close textual analysis: seeing how a narrative is constructed and how a teller rhetorically creates it to make particular points. More recently, he introduced me to critical texts in anthropology, from which I developed the ideas about levels of representation for chapter 1.

In sum, my personal narrative is implicated in this book about narrative analysis. I have a point of view, and a network of relationships that influences the ideas presented here. The approach builds on and extends the Labov-Mishler model and is additionally informed by experiences with literature, sociology, clinical work, teaching, and gender politics. Because of my multidisciplinary identifications, perhaps, I use generic terms and do not emphasize the academic locations of scholars I cite. It is impossible to view any topic from outside, and this volume is no exception.

The book was completed with more than a little help from my friends and colleagues. I thank Virginia Olesen and Adele Clarke for inviting me to present at the 1991 Stone Symposium of the Society for the Study of Symbolic Interaction, where the idea for the book was born. Peter Manning and Marc Miller provided helpful feedback of early drafts, and I was sustained by the support and thoughtful criticism of Susan Bell, Jane Attanucci, and my Philosophical Friends study group. Conversations in a multidisciplinary, multiuniversity Narrative Study Group have shaped my ideas in major ways. Elliot Mishler willingly read draft after draft (expertly typed by Cathie Rocheleau), gave pointed criticism, and pushed me to locate myself. Michelle Huber found and carefully checked every bibliographic reference. Sandra Everson-Jones prepared the figures. Mitch Allen's enthusiasm appeared at just the right moments. Last, but not least, I thank my students. Learning and teaching, and telling and listening, ultimately produced the book.

—Wellfleet, MA

NARRATIVE ANALYSIS

CATHERINE KOHLER RIESSMAN
Boston University

INTRODUCTION: LOCATING NARRATIVE

The study of narrative does not fit neatly within the boundaries of any single scholarly field. Inherently interdisciplinary, it extends the "interpretive turn" in the social sciences (Geertz, 1973, 1983; Rabinow & Sullivan, 1979/1987). As realist assumptions from natural science methods prove limiting for understanding social life, a group of leading U.S. scholars from various disciplines are turning to narrative as the organizing principle for human action (Bruner, 1986, 1990; Cronon, 1992; Rosaldo, 1989; Sarbin, 1986b; Schafer, 1980, 1992). Developments in European theory set the stage for this "narrative turn" (Bakhtin, 1981; Barthes, 1974; Ricoeur, 1981, 1984). Todorov coined the term *narratology* in 1969 in an effort to elevate the form "to the status of an object of knowledge for a new science" (quoted in Godzich, 1989, p. ix).

Story telling, to put the argument simply, is what we do with our research materials and what informants do with us. The story metaphor emphasizes that we create order, construct texts[1] in particular contexts. The mechanical metaphor adopted from the natural sciences (increasingly questioned there) implies that we provide an objective description of forces in the world, and we position ourselves outside to do so.

Narrative analysis takes as its object of investigation the story itself. I limit discussion here to first-person accounts by respondents of their experience, putting aside other kinds of accounts (e.g., our descriptions of what

1

2

happened in the field and other researcher narrativizations, including the "master narratives" of theory).[2] The purpose is to see how respondents in interviews impose order on the flow of experience to make sense of events and actions in their lives. The methodological approach examines the informant's story and analyzes how it is put together, the linguistic and cultural resources it draws on, and how it persuades a listener of authenticity. Analysis in narrative studies opens up the forms of telling about experience, not simply the content to which language refers. We ask, why was the story told *that* way?

Nature and the world do not tell stories, individuals do. Interpretation is inevitable because narratives are representations. There is no hard distinction in postpositivist research between fact and interpretation (Stivers, 1993). Human agency and imagination determine what gets included and excluded in narrativization, how events are plotted, and what they are supposed to mean. Individuals construct past events and actions in personal narratives to claim identities and construct lives.

> How individuals recount their histories—what they emphasize and omit, their stance as protagonists or victims, the relationship the story establishes between teller and audience—all shape what individuals can claim of their own lives. Personal stories are not merely a way of telling someone (or oneself) about one's life; they are the means by which identities may be fashioned. (Rosenwald & Ochberg, 1992b, p. 1)

Not merely information storage devices, narratives structure perceptual experience, organize memory, "segment and purpose–build the very events of a life" (Bruner, 1987, p. 15). Individuals become the autobiographical narratives by which they tell about their lives. These private constructions typically mesh with a community of life stories, "deep structures" about the nature of life itself.

Personal Narratives as Data

Locating narratives of personal experience for analysis is not difficult. They are ubiquitous in everyday life. We can all think of a conversation when someone told in exquisite detail what she said, what he said, what happened next—a recapitulation of every nuance of a moment that had special meaning for her. Psychotherapists encounter narratives of personal experience everyday and use them to change lives by retelling and constructing new and more fulfilling ones (Schafer, 1992; White & Epston,

1990). Telling stories about past events seems to be a universal human activity, one of the first forms of discourse we learn as children (Nelson, 1989) and used throughout the life course by people of all social backgrounds in a wide array of settings. "So natural is the impulse to narrate," wrote H. White (1989), that the form is almost inevitable for any report of how things happened, a solution to "the problem of how to translate *knowing* into *telling*" (p. 1, emphasis in original).

Research interviews are no exception. Respondents (if not interrupted with standardized questions) will hold the floor for lengthy turns and sometimes organize replies into long stories. Traditional approaches to qualitative analysis often fracture these texts in the service of interpretation and generalization by taking bits and pieces, snippets of a response edited out of context. They eliminate the sequential and structural features that characterize narrative accounts (for a critique of mainstream methods that suppress narrative, see Mishler, 1986a).

The precise definition of personal narrative is a subject of debate, to be discussed below. For now, it refers to talk organized around consequential events. A teller in a conversation takes a listener into a past time or "world" and recapitulates what happened then to make a point, often a moral one. In qualitative interviews, typically most of the talk is not narrative but question-and-answer exchanges, arguments, and other forms of discourse.

Respondents narrativize particular experiences in their lives, often where there has been a breach between ideal and real, self and society. Those I studied often told long stories about their marriages to explain their divorces (Riessman, 1990a). Individuals facing the biographic disruption of chronic illness reconstruct a coherent self in narratives (Bury, 1982; Riessman, 1990b; G. Williams, 1984). Embodying the self in stories can occur in settings where the self is being disembodied, such as medical examinations (Young, 1989).

Despite the seeming universality of the discourse form, some experiences are extremely difficult to speak about (Roth, 1993). Political conditions constrain particular events from being narrated. The ordinary response to atrocities is to banish them from awareness (Herman, 1992). Survivors of political torture, war, and sexual crimes silence themselves and are silenced because it is too difficult to tell and to listen. Rape survivors, for example, may not be able to talk about what they experienced as terrorizing violations because others do not regard them as violations. Under these circumstances, women may have difficulty even naming their experience. If it is spoken about, the experience emerges as a kind of "prenarrative: it does not develop or progress in time, and it does not reveal the storyteller's feelings or interpretations of events" (Herman, 1992, p. 175). Social movements aid individuals to name their injuries, connect with others, and engage in political action. Research interviewers can also bear witness. (For an example involving marital rape see Riessman, 1992.)

A primary way individuals make sense of experience is by casting it in narrative form (Bruner, 1990; Gee, 1985; Mishler, 1986a). This is especially true of difficult life transitions and trauma: As Isak Dinesen said, "All sorrows can be borne if we can put them into a story" (quoted in Arendt, 1958, p. 175). Narrators create plots from disordered experience, give reality "a unity that neither nature nor the past possesses so clearly. In so doing, we move well beyond nature into the intensely human realm of value" (Cronon, 1992, p. 1349). Precisely because they are essential meaning-making structures, narratives must be preserved, not fractured, by investigators, who must respect respondents' ways of constructing meaning and analyze how it is accomplished.

Studying Narratives

The idea of telling an informant's story is not new to qualitative sociologists, particularly those from the Chicago School tradition. The Jack Roller (Shaw, 1938) and Doc (Whyte, 1943) are classic characters in American sociology, and their stories have instructed generations of students about urban life (male life, that is; women's is largely invisible in Chicago School ethnographies). What is different about narrative studies, compared to ethnographic accounts and recent approaches to textual analysis?

Traditional ethnographies that incorporate first-person accounts are intended as realistic descriptions, different only in format from other scientific descriptions. Although the rhetoric of writing may vary (Atkinson, 1990; Richardson, 1990; Van Maanen, 1988), it is the "events, not the stories informants create about them, that are intended to command our attention" (Rosenwald & Ochberg, 1992b, p. 2). Language is viewed as a transparent medium, unambiguously reflecting stable, singular meanings.

Critics of the realist assumptions of positivism challenge these views of language and knowing and provide the philosophical underpinnings for narrative studies. Skeptical about a correspondence theory of truth, language is understood as deeply constitutive of reality, not simply a technical device for establishing meaning. Informants' stories do not mirror a world "out there." They are constructed, creatively authored, rhetorical, replete with assumptions, and interpretive.

There are, of course, a variety of approaches to textual analysis in the social sciences, for example, semiotics, hermeneutics, conversational and discourse analysis, and textual approaches to documents. In the humanities, the deconstructive method has spread like wildfire through American departments of literature, and the idea of textual objectivism has been seriously challenged (Fish, 1980). In sociology and psychology, social constructionism (Berger & Luckmann, 1966; Gergen, 1985) is stimulating some to use tools and perspectives from the humanities to examine language, resulting in "blurred genres," to use Geertz's (1983) felicitous phrase. Celebrating this blurring, Gusfield (1989) locates historically this "humanistic" trend for sociologists (but see Eagleton, 1983).

Although narratologists draw some insights from these traditions, the approach is distinguished by an interpretive thrust. Narrative analysis— and there is no *one* method here—has to do with "how protagonists interpret things" (Bruner 1990, p. 51), and we can go about systematically interpreting their interpretations. Because the approach gives prominence to human agency and imagination, it is well suited to studies of subjectivity and identity. It is inappropriate for topics and theories in which the characteristics of actors as active subjects remain unexplored or implicit but well suited to others, including symbolic interaction and feminist studies. Subjectivity, of course, is deeply distrusted in mainstream social science, which values context-free laws and generalized explanations (but see Ellis & Flaherty, 1992; Hollway, 1989). Yet in personal narratives, "it is precisely because of their subjectivity—their rootedness in time, place, and personal experience, in their perspective-ridden character—that we value them" (Personal Narratives Group, 1989b, pp. 263-264).

To the sociologically oriented investigator, studying narratives is additionally useful for what they reveal about social life—culture "speaks itself" through an individual's story. It is possible to examine gender inequalities, racial oppression, and other practices of power that may be taken for granted by individual speakers. Narrators speak in terms that seem natural, but we can analyze how culturally and historically contingent these terms are (Rosenwald & Ochberg, 1992a).

The time is now ripe for a methodological discussion on narrative. There is a burgeoning literature that has touched almost every discipline and profession. No longer the province only of literary study, the "narrative turn" in the human sciences has embraced history (Cronon, 1992; White,

1989), anthropology and folklore (Behar, 1993; Rosaldo, 1989; Shuman, 1986; Young, 1987), psychology (Bruner, 1986, 1990; Cohler, 1982; McCabe & Peterson, 1991; Mishler, 1986a; Polkinghorne, 1988; Rosenwald & Ochberg, 1992a; Sarbin, 1986b), sociology (Boje, 1991; Chase & Bell, in press), and sociolinguistics (Gee, 1986, 1991; Labov, 1982; Polanyi, 1985). Even quantitative researchers are getting on board (Greenley, 1992; Veroff, Sutherland, Chadiha, & Ortega, in press). The professions, too, have discovered narrative: law ("Legal Storytelling," 1989; J. B. White, 1984; P. J. Williams, 1991), medicine (Charon, 1986, 1989; Kleinman, 1988), nursing (Sandelowski, 1991), psychiatry and psychoanalysis (Schafer, 1992; Slavney & McHugh, 1984; Spence, 1982), social work (Laird, 1988, in press), and education (Witherell & Noddings, 1991). The *Journal of Narrative and Life History* publishes research reports.

Organization of the Book

The book is organized into three parts. The first chapter provides theoretical context for the methodological discussion to follow and is composed of two sections. I begin by problematizing the very idea of representing experience. I present research as a series of transformations involving telling, listening, transcribing, analyzing, and reading. I then turn to narrative theory to note key concepts and debates in the field.

Chapter 2 presents actual models of narrative analysis that relate to the theory in Chapter 1. The first example, a woman's life story told to anthropologist Ginsburg, provides a way into the second and third, by sociologists (Bell and myself) who draw on and extend sociolinguistic methods. A certain diversity of approach is emphasized by the three examples, although, as suggested earlier, my location, training, and theoretical precommitments decidedly shape the choice of work and stance toward it. I have a special interest in women's health, and the three examples reflect this substantive interest. I also value "unpacking" a text. Obviously, narrative analysis has applications well beyond medical sociology and women's lives.

Chapter 3 offers practical suggestions for doing narrative work that build on the three examples and cycle back to the theoretical issues in Chapter 1. The book concludes with a brief chapter that outlines two current dilemmas: validation in narrative studies and limitations of the method, including whether it can be combined with other approaches to data.

This is a large vision for such a small book. I cannot represent everything that is important in current work on narrative, which crosses the borders of many academic departments and disciplines. To deepen understanding of ideas I can only touch on here, I hope readers will seek out the many sources provided in the references.

Notes

1. *Text* has multiple meanings in contemporary academic discourse. Learning from a lecture Dorothy Smith gave to the Massachusetts Interdisciplinary Discourse Analysis Seminar (MIDAS) in 1992, I use the word very concretely to refer to work that is reproducible (e.g., transcripts of interviews, drafts, publications).

2. For examples of the latter, see Landau (1984) on evolutionary theory, Cronon (1992) on historical narratives, and Schafer (1992) on psychoanalytical theory.

8

1. THEORETICAL CONTEXTS

It is perhaps a sign of our times that investigators are questioning how we represent life in scientific work (Lynch & Woolgar, 1990). Qualitative researchers often seek to depict others' experiences but act as if representation is not a problem. Feminists, for example, emphasize "giving voice" to previously silenced groups of women by describing the diversity of their experiences (Fonow & Cook, 1991; Gilligan, 1982; Gluck & Patai, 1991; Reinharz, 1992). I share the goal but am more cautious. We cannot give voice, but we do hear voices that we record and interpret. Representational decisions cannot be avoided; they enter at numerous points in the research process, and qualitative analysts including feminists must confront them.

The Representation of Experience

Investigators do not have direct access to another's experience. We deal with ambiguous representations of it—talk, text, interaction, and interpretation. It is not possible to be neutral and objective, to merely represent (as opposed to interpret) the world (Peller, 1987). At the risk of oversimplifying, there are, at a minimum, five levels or kinds of representation in the research process, with porous boundaries between them, depicted in Figure 1.1. (The danger of my representation, of course, is to make the borders more real than semantic.)[3]

To ground what would otherwise be an abstract discussion of the figure, and related interpretive problems, I will make my points inductively and a bit unconventionally. I interweave discussion of the figure with a narrative about an experience on a recent trip to South India.

I went to India to make arrangements for fieldwork I am beginning there on the meaning and management of infertility. For a respite from seemingly endless train rides to meet potential collaborators and locate an appropriate setting for the research, I went to stay for a few days at a tropical resort in Kerala. Early one morning, I took a walk from my hotel, along a deserted beach.

If we adopt the starting point of phenomenology[4] and the lived world of immediate everyday experience, the world of this inhabited beach is " 'already there' before reflection begins—as an inalienable presence" (Merleau-Ponty, 1962/1989, p. vii). Walking at dawn, I encounter it at a prelinguistic realm of experience—images, plays of colors and lights, noises, and fleeting sensations—in the stream of consciousness. I am one with the world and make no distinction at this point between my bodily perceptions and the objects I am conscious of that comprise the beach. Like all social actors, I experience this world from the "natural attitude," taking it for granted, not thinking about and analyzing it (Husserl, 1939/1973; Schutz, 1932/1967).

ATTENDING TO EXPERIENCE

Then I attend to and make discrete certain features in the stream of consciousness—reflecting, remembering, recollecting them into observations. I scan the beach (metaphorically speaking) and isolate certain images, which are known in a given language community by certain words—sunlight, sand, waves, fishing. On this particular occasion, the sound of fishermen chanting is the object I attend to, not the smell of the surf, or the feel of the water—yesterday's images. I stop and watch. Men pull in giant nets, their synchronous movements aided by the rhythmic chant between them. The men in patterned lungis eventually sell the fish to women in brightly colored saris who, placing pails filled with fish on their heads, leave for market. By attending, I make certain phenomena meaningful, the first level of representation in Figure 1.1.[5]

There is choice in what I notice, a selection from the totality of the unreflected on, the primary experience. The truth of hearing and vision predominate over touch and smell, for example. The gendered nature of fishing work also strikes me because of theoretical interests and values. I actively construct reality in new ways at this first level of representation, to myself, by thinking.

TELLING ABOUT EXPERIENCE

Next comes the telling, the performance of a personal narrative. I come back to the United States from India and subsequently relate to friends at dinner the experience of the walk—coming upon the fishermen, their chant, the women, and my marvel. I re-present the events, already ordered to some degree, to these listeners in conversation, with all the opportunities and constraints the form of discourse entails. Although the walk happened many weeks before in another land, I relate it as one inside the experience, enacting the action in a conversation. My account takes the form of a narrative about what happened: I describe waking up early, taking a walk before breakfast, seeing the fishermen, watching as women

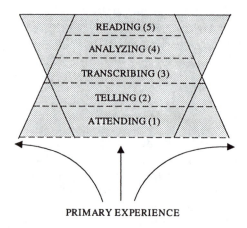

Figure 1.1. Levels of Representation in Research Process

arrived with empty pails, my fascination with the division of labor and women's economic self-sufficiency, in India where women are typically depicted as subservient. I describe the setting, characters, unfolding plot, and stitch the story together in a way that makes my interpretation of the events clear. To capture the moment on that particular morning, I describe at great length the sunlight, the color of the men's lungis and the women's saris, bringing these objects from the real world of the beach to a narrative space in my friends' living room in Cambridge, MA. My rendering draws on resources from my cultural context, notably the gender-based division of labor that all participants in the conversation value as a category of analysis. My friends listen, question, urge me to say more about particular aspects of the exchange between men and women; I, in turn, refashion the events in response to their cues and, to make the importance of the scene real for them, expand on what the moment means in the larger context of my life plans for living and working in India. By talking and listening, we produce a narrative together (Level 2 in Figure 1.1).

In the telling, there is an inevitable gap between the experience as I lived it and any communication about it. Caught in the "prison house of language," in the words of Nietzsche (quoted in Jameson, 1972), there is no way to break through to the ideas to which my words refer because language is "uncommunicative of anything other than itself" (Merleau-

Ponty, 1962/1989, p. 188). Yet, without words, the sounds, movements, and images of the beach experience cease to exist. Language makes them real, as it does the gendered practices of fishing because, as Merleau-Ponty suggested,

> Our linguistic ability enables us to descend into the realm of our primary perceptual and emotional experience, to find there a reality susceptible to verbal understanding, and to bring forth a meaningful interpretation of this primary level of our existence. . . . By finding meaning in experience and then expressing this meaning in words, the speaker enables the community to think about experience and not just live it. (cited in Polkinghorne, 1988, pp. 29-30)

Meaning also shifts in other ways because it is constructed at this second level of representation in a process of interaction. The story is being told to particular people; it might have taken a different form if someone else were the listener. In this case, I am not simply representing the experience on the beach from some neutral place but in a specific conversation with a mentor/friend and his partner, who mean something to me. In telling about an experience, I am also creating a self—how I want to be known by them. Beginning the new research project, my friends have raised questions that have forced me to confront difficult issues, including my position as a privileged, white, Western woman studying South Asian women's health. My rendering of the narrative about the beach scene is colored by this context. Like all social actors, I seek to persuade myself and others that I am a good person. My narrative is inevitably a self representation (Goffman, 1959).

TRANSCRIBING EXPERIENCE

If either of my friends were acting in their roles as social science investigators, they would have taped the conversation. An audio recording would be more selective than a video, of course, but in neither case would the entire conversation be captured. Whatever form of taping used, they would ultimately have to represent it in some kind of text, a "fixation" of action, in the words of Ricoeur, into written speech (cited in Packer & Addison, 1989). Transcribing, the third level of representation in Figure 1.1, is, like the earlier ones, incomplete, partial, and selective.

Millett (1971), early in the contemporary feminist movement, commented on the tape recorder:[6]

Without this device to preserve the very sound of language, we should have no idea of how people *really* talk: their pauses, inflections, emphases, unfinished sentences, short periods. All attempts to mimic spoken language seem terribly mannered, and one comes to respect [Gertrude] Stein still more, and to admire how carefully she must have listened. (p. 32)

Millett discussed the issue of making a written transcription from an audio tape of her interviews with women workers in the sex industry (prostitutes):

What I have tried to capture here is the character of the English I heard spoken by four women and then recorded on tape. I was struck by the eloquence of what was said, and yet when I transcribed the words onto paper, the result was at first disappointing. Some of the wit of M's black and southern delivery had disappeared, gone with the tang of her voice. . . . J's difficulty in speaking of things so painful that she had repressed them for years required that I speak often on her tapes, hoping to give her support, then later, edit myself out. (p. 31)

Millett's solution, in addition to editing herself out, was to do "a good deal of work to transform spoken to linear-language" (p. 32) or to adopt a loose oral narrative and summarize what the women said. In an effort to display a polyphonic text that respected the different voices of the four women, she ultimately displayed the women's talk in her written text in four columns: a quartet in which voices "were instruments expressing their diverse experiences" (p. 33).

Twenty years later, an investigator wanting to "capture" my beach experience faces similar problems, but in the interim a great deal has been written about transcription practices. Transforming spoken language into a written text is now taken quite seriously because thoughtful investigators no longer assume the transparency of language. Qualitative researchers now ask themselves how detailed transcriptions should be. How, for example, could they best capture the rhythm of my talk about the fisherman's chant? Should they include silences, false starts, emphases, nonlexicals like "uhm," discourse markers like "y'know" or "so," overlapping speech, and other signs of listener participation in the narrative? Should they give clauses separate lines and display rhythmic and poetic structures by grouping lines? Not simply technical questions, these seemingly mundane choices of what to include and how to arrange and display the text have serious implications for how a reader will understand the narrative.

There is no one, true representation of spoken language. Mishler (1991b) makes the analogy to photography, which supposedly "pictures reality." Yet the technology of lenses, films, printing papers, and darkroom practices also have made possible an extraordinary diversity of possible images of the same object. The form of representation reflects the artist's views and conceptions—values about what's important. Photographers, like investigators (transcribers), fix the essence of a figure. By denying viewers (readers) information, they paradoxically provide us room to supply our own. We can invent an entire world analyzing the figures (dialogue), although we know very little about them. But I am getting a little ahead of my story.

Transcribing discourse, like photographing reality, is an interpretive practice. Decisions about how to transcribe, like decisions about telling and listening, are theory driven[7] (Ochs, 1979) and rhetorical; by displaying text in particular ways, we provide grounds for our arguments, just like a photographer guides the viewer's eye with lenses and by cropping images. Different transcription conventions lead to and support different interpretations and ideological positions, and they ultimately create different worlds. Meaning is constituted in very different ways with alternative transcriptions of the same stretch of talk (Mishler, 1991b).

ANALYZING EXPERIENCE

A fourth level of representation in Figure 1.1 enters as the investigator explicitly analyzes the transcript,[8] or typically a number of them. Perhaps the research issue is defining critical moments in the awakening of work identity. Like the moment of my walk along the beach, other social scientists narrativize turning points or epiphanies (Denzin, 1988) in their work lives. The challenge is to identify similarities across the moments into an aggregate, a summation. An investigator sits with pages of tape-recorded stories, snips away at the flow of talk to make it fit between the covers of a book, and tries to create sense and dramatic tension. There are decisions about form, ordering, style of presentation, and how the fragments of lives that have been given in interviews will be housed. The anticipated response to the work inevitably shapes what gets included and excluded.[9] In the end, the analyst creates a metastory about what happened by telling what the interview narratives signify, editing and reshaping what was told, and turning it into a hybrid story, a "false document" (Behar, 1993). Values, politics, and theoretical commitments enter once again. Although a kind of betrayal—the beach story and others like it are born again in an alien tongue—it is also necessary and productive; no matter how talented the original storyteller was, a life story told in conversation certainly does not come ready-made as a book (Behar, 1993), an article, or a dissertation. The stop-and-start style of oral stories of personal experience gets pasted together into something different.

READING EXPERIENCE

The fifth and final level of representation in Figure 1.1 comes as the reader encounters the written report. Perhaps an early draft was circulated to colleagues and their comments were incorporated into the so-called final product,[10] or perhaps published work was returned to the people it is about, who may or may not recognize their experience in it or like how they are portrayed. In any case, translations of my original narrative about an experience in India and analytic work on what it means by my social scientist friends in Cambridge inevitably gets into the hands of others, who bring their own meanings to bear. An extract about a beach walk might give some readers a shiver of recognition, whereas others might wonder about my relationship with my subjects—men and women of the fishing village in Kerala. What does my presence as a white English-speaking woman signify, given that Malayalam is the native tongue? How are race and class inscribed in the text?[11] It might be difficult, if not impossible, to get answers to these and similar questions. All a reader has is the analyst's representation.

Every text is "plurivocal, open to several readings and to several constructions" (Rabinow & Sullivan, 1979/1987, p. 12). Even for the same reader, a work can provoke quite different readings in different historical contexts (imagine Flaubert's *Madame Bovary*, for example, before and after the recent feminist movement). Collaboration is inevitable because the reader is an agent of the text (Bruner, 1986). Critical readers include their understandings of the "makings" of a work in their interpretations of it. Because a writer cannot tell all (seemingly irrelevant personal and historical circumstances have been excluded), interpretation may focus on how power and history work through a supposedly objective text. Readers raise historical contingencies and excluded standpoints—of women, people of color, non-Western views—as they dislodge the seemingly secure ground under our representations. Written texts are created within, and against, particular traditions and audiences, and these contexts can be brought to bear by readers. The point is that all texts stand on moving ground; there is no master narrative (Clifford, 1986; Clifford & Marcus, 1986; Sosnoski, 1991).

Ultimately, it is unclear who really authors a text, although Western texts come with individual authors' names penned to them. The meaning of a text is always meaning to someone. The truths we have constructed "are meaningful to specific interpretive communities in limiting historical circumstances" (Clifford, 1988, p. 112). Any finding—a depiction of a culture, psychological process, or social structure—exists in historical time, between subjects in relations of power. Whereas traditional social science has claimed to represent the experiences of populations and cultures, the new criticism states that we cannot speak, finally and with ultimate authority, for others. Our subjects "do not hold still for their portraits" (Clifford, 1986, p. 10; see also Wolf, 1992, regarding how feminists have been making similar postmodern arguments for some time).

THE LIMITS OF REPRESENTATION

Generalizing from my beach walk and its repeated transformations, there are implications for research practices. All forms of representation of experience are limited portraits. Simply stated, we are interpreting and creating texts at every juncture, letting symbols stand for or take the place of the primary experience, to which we have no direct access. Meaning is ambiguous because it arises out of a process of interaction between people: self, teller, listener and recorder, analyst, and reader. Although the goal may be to tell the whole truth, our narratives about others' narratives are our worldly creations. There is no "view from no where" (Nagel, 1986), and what might have seemed nowhere in the past is likely to be somewhere in the present or future. Meaning is fluid and contextual, not fixed and universal. All we have is talk and texts that represent reality partially, selectively, and imperfectly.

Each level in the Figure 1.1 involves an expansion but also a reduction: Tellers select features from the "whole" experience to narrate but add other interpretative elements. A similar process occurs with transcribing, analyzing, and reading. Framing discussion of the research process in the language of "representation" rather than as "stages" or "perspectives" emphasizes that we actively make choices that can be accomplished in different ways.[12] Obviously, the agency of the teller is central to composing narratives from personal experience, but so are the actions of others—listener, transcriber, analyst, and reader.

The idea of representation brings into view the constructed nature of social scientific work. Said (1979) went even further, and his views have bearing for all researchers:

> [The] real issue is whether indeed there can be a true representation of anything, or whether any and all representations, because they are representations, are embedded first in the language and then in the culture, institutions, and political ambience of the representor. If the latter alternative is the correct one (as I believe it is), then we must be prepared to accept the fact that a representation is *eo ipso* implicated, intertwined, embedded, interwoven with a great many other things besides the "truth," which is itself a representation. (pp. 272-273)

Whether we accept ultimate relativism, awareness of levels of representation presses us to be more conscious, reflective, and cautious about the claims we make.

Returning to the issue of giving voice to women's experience, I prefer to think of research as a chorus of voices, with an embedded contrapuntal duet (Gorelick, 1991). There are strains because most researchers are privileged and white and many women we want to include are not. Some voices will have to be restrained to hear voices from below (Rollins, 1985) to create a particular harmony, but a different interpreter might well allow other voices to dominate.[13]

Representing women's experience is limited further because language is often inadequate (DeVault, 1990), and the world as perceived by subjects may be confined and organized by structures of oppression not apparent to participants themselves (Gorelick, 1991; Smith, 1987).[14] Just as gender is not enough in feminist research (Riessman, 1987), giving voice to experience is not either, even as we commit to women's standpoints. Interpreting experience—and this happens at all five levels in Figure 1.1 —involves representing reality; we create and recreate voices over and over again during the research process. Nowhere is this more evident than in studies of personal narratives.

Narratives as Representations

I now look more closely at the levels of telling/transcribing/analyzing as they are discussed in narrative theory. The literature is vast, and I enter the field through a path cleared by others, especially Langellier (1989), Martin (1986), and Mishler (1986a). There is no binding theory of narrative but instead great conceptual diversity. My limited aim here is to identify key concepts, debates, and interpretive dilemmas that anyone doing research with first-person accounts of experience will have to consider and to provide resources. I make my own position clear in Chapters 2 and 3, when discussing examples of narrative studies and the specifics of doing the work.

WHAT IS A NARRATIVE?

There is considerable disagreement about the precise definition of narrative. Among one group the definition is so overly broad to include just about anything. In the clinical literature, for example, there is reference to illness narratives, life stories, and narration in psychotherapy about the past. However compelling narrative may be as a metaphor for telling about lives, systematic methods of analysis and detailed transcriptions are often lacking. The definition of narrative has been quite restrictive among another group. Labov (1972), in particular, assumes all narratives are stories about a specific past event, and they have common properties (described below). Most scholars treat narratives as discrete units, with clear beginnings and endings, as detachable from the surrounding discourse rather than as situated events.

In *Poetics*, Aristotle said that a narrative has a beginning, middle, and end. Ever since, scholars agree that sequence is necessary, if not sufficient, for narrative (on chronicles, see Cronon, 1992; Polanyi, 1985). Labov and Waletzky (1967) argued that stories follow a chronological sequence: The order of events moves in a linear way through time and the "order cannot be changed without changing the inferred sequence of events in the original semantic interpretation" (p. 21). A narrative, according to this definition, is always responding to the question "and then what happened?" Western assumptions about time marching forward underpin Labov's approach. Young (1987) argued for consequential sequencing: One event causes another in the narrative, although the links may not always be chronological (also see Culler, 1980). Still others argue for thematic sequencing: An episodic narrative is stitched together by theme rather than by time (Michaels, 1981). Western, white, middle-class interviewers seem to expect temporally sequenced plots and have trouble hearing ones that are organized episodically (Riessman, 1987).

In conversation, tellers sometimes let listeners know a story is coming and indicate when it is over, with entrance and exit talk (Jefferson, 1979).

18

"Once upon a time" and "they lived happily ever after" are classic examples in folktales of bracketing devices. But stories told in research interviews are rarely so clearly bounded, and locating them is often a complex interpretive process. Where one chooses to begin and end a narrative can profoundly alter its shape and meaning.[15] Decisions underscore how deeply the listener/interpreter is part of the text.

Not all narratives in interviews are stories in the linguistic sense of the term. Individuals relate experiences using a variety of narrative genres (Riessman, 1991). We recognize a genre by the persistence of certain conventional elements (Mitchell, 1990), which engage us in quite different ways. When we hear stories, for instance, we expect protagonists, inciting conditions, and culminating events. But not all narratives (or all lives) take this form. Some other genres include habitual narratives (when events happen over and over and consequently there is no peak in the action), hypothetical narratives (which depict events that did not happen), and topic-centered narratives (snapshots of past events that are linked thematically). Genres of narrative, with their distinctive styles and structures, are modes of representation that tellers choose (in concert with listeners' expectations, of course) just as filmmakers decide, based on their intentions and the market, what form the script will take, and what conventions will be used to represent character and action. Different genres persuade differently; they make us care about a situation to varying degrees as they pull us into the teller's point of view (Riessman, 1991).

NARRATIVE STRUCTURES

Like weight bearing walls, personal narratives depend on certain structures to hold them together. Stories told in conversation share common parameters, although they may be put together in contrasting ways and, as a result, point to different interpretations. Events become meaningful because of their placement in a narrative.

Labov's (1972, 1982; Labov & Waletzky, 1967) structural approach is paradigmatic: Most investigators cite it, apply it, or use it as a point of departure (Langellier, 1989). Narratives, he argues, have formal properties and each has a function. A "fully formed" one includes six common elements: an abstract (summary of the substance of the narrative), orientation (time, place, situation, participants), complicating action (sequence of events), evaluation (significance and meaning of the action, attitude of the narrator), resolution (what finally happened), and coda (returns the perspective to the present). With these structures, a teller constructs a story from a primary experience and interprets the significance of events in clauses and embedded evaluation. Using Labov's structural categories to analyze the story of a teacher/parent, Attanucci (1991) shows how multiple interpretations of the moral dilemma he relates are possible. Dichotomous formulations like justice and care (Gilligan, 1982; Brown, Tappan, Gilligan, Miller, & Argyris, 1989) ignore the ambiguities of language that attention to structure brings into view.

Burke's (1945) classic method of analyzing language—dramatism—offers another structural approach that has potential application to a variety of types of narrative, including stories. The grammatical resources that individuals employ to tell persuasive tales are contained in a pentad of terms: act, scene, agent, agency, purpose. "Any complete statement about motives will offer *some kind of* answer to these five questions: What was done (act), when or where it was done (scene), who did it (agent), how he [or she] did it (agency), and why (purpose)" (Burke, 1945, p. xv). Using Burke's grammar to make sense of the contrasting accounts husbands and wives told about a violent incident in marriage, Hydén (1992) shows how male perpetrators favored words that emphasize purpose (*why* he acted as he did), whereas wives emphasize agency (*how* he beat her) and the consequences of the act, both physical and emotional. Hydén relates these language differences to broader themes about the social construction of gender in violent marriages.

Still another approach to structure is represented by Gee (1986), who attends to how a story is said. Drawing on the oral rather than text-based tradition in sociolinguistics, he analyzes changes in pitch, pauses, and other features that punctuate speech that allow interpreters to hear groups of lines together. Using poetic units, stanzas, and strophes to examine the talk of a woman hospitalized for schizophrenia, he shows how organized, coherent, and senseful her speech is (Gee, 1991).[16]

FORMS OF TELLING: CONTEXT AND MEANING

Narrativization tells not only about past actions but how individuals understand those actions, that is, meaning. Plots vary in type: tragedy, comedy, romance, and satire (H. White, 1973). Tellers pour their ordinary lives into these archetypal forms.

Narrators indicate the terms on which they request to be interpreted by the styles of telling they choose. Something said in a whisper, after a long pause, has a different import than the same words said loudly, without a pause. Tellers use elongated vowels, emphasis, pitch, repetition, and other devices to indicate what is important. Emotion is also carried in these and other audible aspects, although much more research is needed on how affect enters into a narrative. Forms of transcription that neglect features of speech miss important information.

Labov's (1972, 1982; Labov & Waletzky, 1967) structures provide another way into the interpretation of meaning. Narrators say in evaluation clauses (the soul of the narrative) how they want to be understood and what the point is. Every good narrator tries to defend against the implicit accusation of a pointless story, warding off the question: "So what?" In evaluation clauses, which typically permeate the narrative, a teller stands back from the unfolding action and tells how he or she has chosen to interpret it (but see Culler, 1980; Toolan, 1988). Representing a narrative about a moral dilemma with and without the evaluation clauses, Attanucci (1991) displayed how interpretation shifts; "evaluation infuses the account with values and meaning" (p. 323). Access to these and other structures that carry meaning depends on how we, as analysts, create texts from talk: representing speech in continuous lines compared to clauses that allow for structural analysis (Level 3 in Figure 1.1).

Narrative theorists disagree on the importance of the interview context (Level 2) in the analysis of narrative (Level 4). Labov's model leaves out the relationship of teller and listener: "His assumption [is] that narrative is a relation among clauses rather than an interaction among participants" (Langellier, 1989, p. 248). At the other extreme is the Personal Narratives Group (1989b), who examine power relations in the production of personal narratives: Who asks the questions and for what purpose? Some narrative analysts, as detailed below, bring the interviewer into the analysis by including his or her guiding questions, nonlexical utterances, and other signs of puzzlement and understanding (Paget, 1983), showing how meaning is interactionally accomplished. Labov avoided the question of whether a "story is being told primarily in order to report a sequence of events or in order to tell a tellable story" (Culler, 1980, p. 36). Viewing story telling as a kind of performance (Goffman, 1974; Toolan, 1988), a teller has a fundamental problem: how to convince a listener who was not there that something important happened. In divorce narratives, for example, individuals tell about times in their troubled marriages and persuade through rhetorically effective forms of symbolic expression—how they craft their tales in collaboration with a listener—that the decision to divorce was justified (Riessman, 1990a). Language, as Burke (1950) said, "is not merely descriptive . . . not just trying to tell people how things are. . . . [I]t is trying to *move people*" (p. 41).

Language has three analytically distinct but interdependent functions (Halliday, 1973), and all are essential for the interpretation of meaning. The ideational function expresses the referential meaning of what is said: "content in terms of the speaker's experience and that of the speech community" (p. 37). The interpersonal function concerns the role relationships between speakers, which allows for the expression of social and personal relations through talk. The textual function refers to structure, how parts of a text are connected syntactically and semantically. Meaning is conveyed at all three levels, although the ideational function tends to dominate communication, that is, informational content about people, situations, and ideas that speakers mean their words to convey. But the meaning of what someone says is not simply its content (ideational); how something is said (textual) in the context of the shifting roles of speaker and listener (interpersonal) is critical also. Narrative analysis provides methods for examining, and relating, meaning at all three levels.

The larger social context is important, too, although scholars differ in the extent to which they include it. At one extreme are the conversation analysts (who rarely include anything as long as a narrative in their samples of talk); focus is limited to what participants say and do in a particular interaction. For the Personal Narratives Group (1989b), context is multilayered, involving the historical moment of the telling, the race, class, and gender systems that narrators manipulate to survive and within which their talk has to be interpreted. My preference sides very much with the latter position; the divorce narratives, for example, would have been impossible to interpret without reference to social discourses and politics, specifically, the transformations in marriage and gender relations of the last 150 years. Women and men made sense of their divorces in narratives that contained assumptions about how marital interactions are supposed to occur in the late-20th-century America. The text is not autonomous of its context.

NARRATIVE TRUTHS

Finally, I touch on a thorny problem in narrative research: the truth of what a teller says. The earlier discussion of representation and Figure 1.1 suggest how excruciatingly complex the issue is; we cannot rely on the posture of descriptive realism or external criteria, as in positivist methods. Sarbin (1986a) called narrative a root metaphor:

> a way of organizing episodes, actions, and accounts of actions; it is an achievement that brings together mundane facts and fantastic creations; time and place are incorporated. The narrative allows for the inclusion of actors' reasons for their acts, as well as the causes of happening. (p. 9)

Narrative analysts, in practice, approach the issue of truth differently. Some assume that language represents reality: The narrative clauses recapitulate experience in the same order as the original events (Labov & Waletzky, 1967). Others, influenced by phenomenology, take the position that narrative constitutes reality: It is in the telling that we make real phenomena in the stream of consciousness (see Young, 1987, pp. 186-210). Still others, interested in the persuasive aspects of language, argue that narrators inscribe into their tales their ideologies and interests (for review see Langellier, 1989). Veroff et al. (in press), for example, interviewed newly married couples and argued that husbands and wives narrate fictions that they present to a listener. These fictions, in turn, "may be the inspirations for acting out a happy or unhappy married life" (p. 9).

The Personal Narratives Group (1989a) wrote of truths in a way that echos my position:

> When talking about their lives, people lie sometimes, forget a lot, exaggerate, become confused, and get things wrong. Yet they *are* revealing truths. These truths don't reveal the past "as it actually was," aspiring to a standard of objectivity. They give us instead the truths of our experiences. . . . Unlike the Truth of the scientific ideal, the truths of personal narratives are neither open to proof nor self-evident. We come to understand them only through interpretation, paying careful attention to the contexts that shape their creation and to the world views that inform them. Sometimes the truths we see in personal narratives jar us from our complacent security as interpreters "outside" the story and make us aware that our own place in the world plays a part in our interpretation and shapes the meanings we derive from them. (p. 261)

Narratives are interpretive and, in turn, require interpretation: They do not "speak for themselves," or "provide direct access to other times, places, or cultures" (p. 264). Our analytic interpretations are partial, alternative truths that aim for "believability, not certitude, for enlargement of understanding rather than control" (Stivers, 1993, p. 424). I return to the issue of validation in the conclusion.

The debates in narrative studies just summarized provide important background for what follows. I draw on relevant facets—definition of a narrative, attention to structure, meaning and context—at the same time as I adopt an interpretive view.

Notes

3. Figure 1.1 is a heuristic, a very imperfect visual representation of my argument. At each level, there is both an addition and a reduction. A student suggested a spiral to depict the process, rather than a series of steps. An editor suggested a sixth level to the figure—re-reading—which is an interesting idea that I entertain when discussing *Madame Bovary*. Visual representations are always partial, incomplete, and limited (Lynch & Woolgar, 1990).

4. Phenomenology is not a uniform philosophical discipline. I am drawing primarily on the work of Husserl, Schutz, and Merleau-Ponty and cannot represent here the many distinctions and differences of emphasis within the movement. For a review, see Stewart and Mickunas (1990).

5. Whether there is raw meaning in the primary experience is a point of difference between Schutz and Merleau-Ponty. There is also considerable debate among scholars about whether language is added after the image (one sees through words to the designated objects) or whether language is inseparable from perceptions, meaning, and social practice. That experience is entirely an artifact of language is an extreme statement of the latter view—a position I am not taking here. For a review of the various positions on language, reality, and meaning in narrative work, see Polkinghorne (1988, pp. 23-31).

6. I thank Susan Bell for bringing to my attention the relevance of Millett's (1971) work for a discussion of transcription practices.

7. *Theory* is not only something academics construct. I am using the term as phenomenologists, such as Schutz (1932/1967), and feminists, such as Smith (1987) and Sosnoski (1991), do: Knowledge found in the ordinary thinking of people in everyday life.

8. As noted above, a transcription is already an interpretation. See Mishler (1991a).

9. Restrictions are now placed by indigenous governments on fieldwork, which "condition in new ways what can, and especially cannot, be said about particular peoples" (Clifford & Marcus, 1986, p. 9).

10. Early readers play crucial roles in the stories about stories that we tell (see Cronon, 1992).

11. For an example involving gender, consider Geertz's (1973) ethnography of Balinese society. The portrait of the cock fight is about men. Balinese women, and Geertz's wife, get marginalized early in his account. When he interprets the society, he may or may not be extending his points to women. We cannot know, but we can ask and question the examples he chooses.

12. I thank Cheryl Hyde for the insight that my language for the problems of research ("representation") emphasizes choice, the investigator's agency.

13. See Behar (1993) for an example of how class and race cleavages between women (investigator and subject) can be brought into the analysis and thicken it. See hooks (1989) for an articulate feminist voice.

14. Yet there is a danger, particularly in comparative research on gender, of imposing categories derived from Western feminist thought onto non-Western women. I am wary of this new form of Western cultural imperialism.

15. For an example from historical research of inclusion and exclusion of Native Americans in narratives about the Great Plains, see Cronon (1992).

16. Other investigators have also attended to poetic devices in ordinary discourse (see Richardson, 1992; Tannen, 1990).

2. PRACTICAL MODELS

I now turn to examples of narrative studies. The three investigators examine women's health concerns and use women's first-person accounts of experience as their primary source of information. I explore how each approaches her text in light of the theoretical contexts of Chapter 1—levels of representation and debates in narrative theory. The "democratic" organization is a deliberate choice, and underscores how there is no single method of narrative analysis but a spectrum of approaches to texts that take narrative form. Whatever their differences (and I make my preferences clear), the examples show that there are ways to analyze individuals' recollections of the past systematically, informed by narrative theory.

Ginsburg studied activists in an abortion struggle and, drawing on a plot-story distinction, analyzed how plot twists in accounts distinguished pro-choice from right-to-life women. Bell studied DES daughters and in a case study, drawing on the structural approaches of Labov and Mishler, she showed how a woman transforms the meaning of her exposure and becomes political. I studied divorce narratives and analyze here, drawing on the poetic structural approach of Gee, the account of a woman who is depressed. The first example explores the broad contours of a life story, the second the linked stories in a single interview, and the third the poetic features embedded in a personal narrative.

Beyond their methodological and substantive differences, the three investigators share some commonalities: All identify as feminists, bring feminist politics to bear to interpret their texts, and open up the difficult problem of representing women's experience. All emphasize women's agency and subjectivity. All hint at broader theoretical questions of why and how women do or do not become politically active.

Methodologically, each example raises a set of questions about how we represent experience in our research reports:

1. How is talk transformed into a written text and how are narrative segments determined?
2. What aspects of the narrative constitute the basis for interpretation?
3. Who determines what the narrative means and are alternative readings possible?

Not the only important questions, I chose these three to open up key methodological decisions hidden in each report that reflect back on the levels of representation identified in Figure 1.1. As Kuhn (1962/1970) argued, exemplars contain much tacit knowledge.

I begin with an example that looks at individuals' talk about their experience and that explicitly adopts narrative language to do so. However, the analytic work that narrative theory presupposes is largely invisible in the first example. I include it, even though quite different from the other two, because it offers important insights that future investigators can extend and expand on.

A Life Story

Anthropologist Ginsburg (1989a, 1989b) studied the lives of 35 women activists in Fargo, ND, who had much in common but who split on the issue of abortion.[17] The community had become painfully divided, and Ginsburg wanted to identify what distinguished right-to-life from pro-choice women. They seemed to share many personal characteristics, religious values, and lives in traditional families, and Ginsburg became interested in how political positions on the abortion issue were linked to personal experiences with family. She saw women activists on both sides of the debate as agents of social transformation and needed a method that attended to the capacity of individuals to explain why they act as they do. Her solution was to generate "life stories in the field and . . . a narrative approach to interpret them" (Ginsburg, 1989a, p. ix). She adopted the everyday meaning of "story," but did not assume a correspondent relationship between what the women told and actual experience or behavior. Instead, she explored how women constructed their positions narratively, how accounts by pro-choice activists compared linguistically and substantively with those of right-to-life women.

NARRATIVE METHOD

In extensive qualitative interviews, Ginsburg observed that both groups of women told "procreation stories" that centered on moments of individual transformation, crises in which the conditions they faced as mothers and available resources were at odds. Stories gave shape to "disorderly" experiences, as narrative theory would predict. Women reported catalyzing experiences through which their political consciousness was fundamentally changed.

Transcript 2.1 displays Ginsburg's analysis of Kay's life story, one of the "compelling texts" that illustrates the general pattern found in other pro-choice interviews. (For a longer version, see Ginsburg, 1989a, pp. 150-155.) Consistent with the rhetorical conventions of the life story method (Bertaux & Kohli, 1984), the text Ginsburg created to represent Kay's life is a mixture of direct quotes (generally brief) from the interview, longer summaries of the content of speech, Ginsburg's statements about theoretical issues, and key substantive themes that cut across the 35 interviews ("Like almost *all* of the women activists . . ."). Ginsburg's authorial voice and interpretive commentary knit the disparate elements together and determine how readers are to understand Kay Ballard's experience. In this form of representation, it is the writer's authority that is privileged, the fourth level of representation in Figure 1.1 (Bell, 1991).

Looking at the interview excerpts I have marked in Ginsberg's text, there are a number of typical narrative features. Whatever the order of telling in the interview might have been—people do not always begin at the beginning—Ginsburg's representation of Kay's experience moves through time. She configures the excerpts so that Kay moves through experiences with natal family, conjugal family, and up to her current activism. The first excerpt tells of the preacher's daughter, early encounters with his "difference," and her identification with him. The next excerpt moves forward to Kay's adulthood, being a mother, and the difficulties doing it full-time ("my mind was a wasteland"). A key moment in self-transformation comes in the third excerpt, a reported conversation with a friend about La Leche League and a flashback to her first birth experience. Kay's consciousness is changed about how childbirth could be different, and she extends her new consciousness to other issues of women's health, specifically women's relationships with their doctors, in the fourth excerpt. The fifth excerpt jumps forward in time (Kay now has four young children), when she has an abortion so they can "make it" as a family. The last two excerpts are not about events but comment on the centrality of religious and ethical principles in Kay's life. She speaks of her many similarities with her political opponents; yet her position cannot exist without a real or imagined other—the opponents to abortion ("them"). The dual themes of difference and sameness give a measure of coherence to Kay's experience, as Ginsburg represents it, beginning and ending the life story.

Attention to sequence is what distinguishes Ginsburg's analytic strategy from traditional ethnographic approaches. She analyzes the unfolding

The central figure of the current controversy in Fargo is Kay Bellevue, the woman who opened the abortion clinic in 1981. Kay grew up in the Midwest, the oldest of seven children. Her father was a Baptist minister; her mother was a homemaker and part-time worker in the public school system. As is the case for many of the pro-choice activists, Kay began her narrative with the biographical "reasons" that, in her view, made her different. The plot begins with this early sense of differentiation, the source of identification with a key family member who served as a model for what she sees as her later oppositional stance toward the culture:

I always perceived myself as different from other kids. As a preacher's kid, whether it was true or not, I always felt people expected me to be perfect and to behave in a ladylike manner. . . . My dad was always interested in what was going on politically and took a keen interest in the antiwar movement and rights for blacks. I was the apple of his eye, and he's always been proud of the things I've done. My dad's a real independent person, and I see a lot of that in me. **Excerpt 1**

In her senior year of college, Kay got pregnant and married, and soon after she moved to Denver, where her husband was pursuing graduate studies in English. Like almost *all* of the women activists, regardless of their position on abortion, Kay's transition to motherhood was an event surrounded by ambivalence. Although her behavior was not in fact that different from that of many right-to-life women—i.e., as a young mother she worked part-time and became involved in community associations—Kay's *interpretation* of her actions stresses the limitations of motherhood. Her plot turns on her unexpected reaction to her assigned and chosen role as mother.

I enjoyed being home, but I could never stay home all the time. I have never done that in my life. After being home one year and taking care of a kid, I felt my mind was a wasteland. And we were so poor we could almost never go out together. **Excerpt 2**

By contrast, pro-life women faced with the same dilemmas emphasize the drawbacks of the workplace. Not surprisingly, for both groups of women, voluntary work for "cause" was an acceptable and satisfying way of managing to balance the pleasures and duties of motherhood with the structural isolation of that work as it is organized in America. For example, La Leche League, an international organization promoting breastfeeding and natural childbirth, is a group where one stands an equal chance of running into a pro-life or pro-choice woman. In her early twenties, Kay became active in a local chapter of La Leche League. In Kay's case, she met a woman who introduced her to feminism, a critical twist in the plot that sets it in tension with the "story." She marks this as a key event.

I met someone who said, "You should come to a La Leche League meeting with me because one of their sessions is on prepared childbirth, and after your experience, you

Transcript 2.1. Kay Ballard's Life Story

SOURCE: Adapted from Personal Narratives Group (1989b). Reprinted by permission of Indiana University Press.

might appreciate hearing what they're talking about." My first child had not been a pleasant birth experience, so I went and I was really intrigued. There were people talking about his childbirth experience like it was the most fantastic thing you'd ever been through. I certainly didn't feel that way. I had a very long labor. I screamed, I moaned. . . . My husband thought I was dying. So anyway, this group introduced me to a whole different conception of childbirth, and my second experience was so different I couldn't believe it. **Excerpt 3**

Kay's growing sense of consciousness concerning the way women's reproductive needs were mishandled by the medical profession crystallized during her third pregnancy.

The way I came to feminism was that through all of this, I became acutely aware of how little physicians who were supposed to be doctors for women actually knew about women's bodies. So I became a real advocate for women to stand up for their rights, starting with breast feeding. **Excerpt 4**

The concerns she gives voice to are not so different from those articulated by her neighbors and fellow citizens who so vehemently oppose her work. In 1972, Kay moved to Fargo because of her husband's job. She joined and continued as a leader in La Leche and got pregnant again. Kay marks this period as one of crisis. Her parents were divorcing, and one of her children was having problems.

Then I ended up having an abortion myself. My youngest was eighteen months old, and I accidentally got pregnant. We had four small kids at the time, and we decided if we were going to make it a family unit, we had all the stress we could tolerate if we were going to survive. **Excerpt 5**

In her more public role, as in the case of her personal decisions regarding abortion, Kay always linked her activism to a strong commitment to ethical principles and strong family ties.

I have always acted on what to me are Judeo-Christian principles. The Ten Commandments plus "Love thy neighbor." I was raised by my family to have a very, very strong sense of ethics, and it's still with me. **Excerpt 6**

I think it's easy for them to stereotype us as having values very different from theirs, and that's not the case at all. Many of the people who get abortions have values very similar to the antiabortion people. The right-to-life people don't know how deeply I care for my own family and how involved I am, since I have four children and spent the early years of my life working for a breastfeeding organization. **Excerpt 7** plot of her informants' presentations. Elaborating on a framework developed by the Russian formalist Viktor Sklovskij, Ginsburg notes the difference between the story and the plot in narrative. The story (*fabula*) is the raw, temporally sequenced, or causal narrative of a life, the "expected arrangement of a woman's biography according to Western narrative and social conventions" (Ginsburg, 1989b, p. 64); one is born, grows up like other children, marries, becomes a mother, and so on. The plot (*sjuzet*) emerges from the "unexpected twists in the narrative that draw attention to differences from the conventional story" (Ginsburg, 1989a, p. 142); one is different from other children, pregnancy happens before marriage, not all pregnancies are welcomed, and so on. Both pro-choice and right-to-life women constructed plots out of stories, in which "the social consequences of different definitions of the female life course in contemporary America are selected, rejected, reordered, and reproduced in a new form" (Ginsburg, 1989b, p. 64). But the two groups of women constructed their plot lines in very different ways. Kay illustrates the typical pro-choice plot line: being different in childhood (Excerpt 1); questioning the confines of motherhood through a particular reproductive experience (Excerpt 2); a conversion upon contact with feminism in the 1960s and 1970s (Excerpts 3 and 4); and a subsequent reframing of understandings of self, women's interests, and ideals of nurturance (Excerpts 4-7).

Generalizing from Ginsburg's method, a comparison of plot lines across a series of first-person accounts is one way to approach narratives. The analyst examines causal sequence to locate the turning points that signal a break between ideal and real, the cultural script and the counternarrative. The investigator searches for similarities and differences among the sample in discursive strategies—how the story is told in the broadest sense. (For another example, see Chase & Bell, in press). Illustrative quotes from the interview provide evidence for the investigator's interpretation of the plot twists, deviations from the conventional story.

QUESTIONS

Turning to my first questions, how has Ginsburg transformed the women activists' talk into written text, and how are narrative segments determined? She did not discuss transcription conventions, how the conversations she had with women activists were represented, that is, transformed from Level 2 to Level 3 in Figure 1.1. These aspects of the analytic process are invisible to view. As is typical in the life story approach, the focus is on summarizing the gist of what Kay said; the transition from spoken to written language is assumed to be unproblematic. Talk is "cleaned up" of disfluencies to render it easily readable. Language is viewed as a transparent medium, useful primarily to get to underlying content.

Ginsburg (1989a) did not define what she meant by narrative. She referred to "procreation stories . . . in which women use their activism to frame and interpret their historical and biographical experiences" (p. 134). In her usage, life story and narrative are synonymous, a loose and broad definition that Ginsburg shares with others in the life story tradition (Bruner, 1990; McAdams & Ochberg, 1988). The entire interview implicitly constitutes the narrative. In another sense, the excerpts are not narratives, at least as understood in narrative theory; they do not pull the reader into the gritty detail of the past but instead summarize and gloss past events and actions.

Ginsburg was sensitive to the historical context that gave rise to Kay's and other informants' accounts but not to interview context. We do not know, for example, about the nature of the interaction that produced Kay's narrative and are not shown examples of actual dialogues. Ginsburg (1989a) said, "My objective was to interfere as little as possible in the creation of the narrative" (p. 135), implying she was ferreting out data that had a prior existence in the recesses of the informant's memory, although elsewhere she is careful to distinguish between the story and the prior experience to which it refers.

Personal narratives are produced in conversation; Kay's is the product of a particular interview context, a dialogue between a particular teller and listener in a relation of power, at a particular historical moment. Elsewhere, in a section titled "Fieldwork: The Observer Observed," Ginsburg (1989a, pp. 4-6) offered important insights about how her outsider status influenced the research process, but in the analysis of the narratives she edited herself out. The second level of representation in Figure 1.1, the way the two women are constructing a text together, is not brought into view.[18]

Second, what aspects of the narrative constitute the basis for interpretation? Ginsburg constructed her interpretation of Kay's life story from the whole interview. Yet readers only see brief excerpts, snapshots, or moments in the woman's life that are chosen and arranged to represent the conversion from Baptist preacher's daughter to abortion activist. We have to take the author's word that the life story is sequenced as she says because we cannot see very much of it. In this way, Ginsburg used interview material much like traditional qualitative analysts, taking bits and pieces, snippets of a response, that supported her evolving theory. She attended to the plot twists within the life story, but it is not entirely clear what constitutes a plot twist, and she did not provide enough information for a structural analysis. The author interprets the story for readers, refuses to allow it to speak, ambiguously, for itself.

I wonder, for example, what Kay means when she says in the second excerpt that "her mind was a wasteland." She could be describing the chronic understimulation that many mothers of young children feel: Her intellect is being wasted with full-time motherhood. Or "wasteland" could carry other meanings. Kay's word choice here is unusual, with referents in poetry (T. S. Eliot), environmental studies, perhaps to the landscape of Fargo itself. Is she referring to her social isolation in a traditional family? I find myself having to appropriate the term into prior understandings, absorb it to my meanings, my life (the fifth level of representation), which may not be what Kay had in mind at all. Those who collect personal narratives, unlike historians who work with archival materials, can ask informants what they mean by what they say. Language used in an interview can be scrutinized—"unpacked," not treated as self-evident, transparent, unambiguous—during the interview itself as well as later, in the analysis of interview transcripts.

Finally, who determines what Kay's narrative means? Whose story is it? Consistent with the norms for ethnographic writing, persuasive power is in Ginsburg's text, the fourth level of representation—her generalizations about what women said and what it means. She chose particular excerpts to display her interpretive framework, but the analysis is not closely tied to specifics of the activists' accounts. The structure of Ginsburg's text privileges the author's interpretation, that is, weaves Kay's narrative into Ginsburg's narrative about historical change. Although the aim was to understand "the abortion controversy from the actor's point of view" (Ginsburg, 1989a, p. 3), readers are constantly directed by the author's interpretive voice. This is a translated text, an in-between genre, a mediated life story narrative (Peacock, 1992). Kay's talk functions as proof of an argument, brought to bear as one might use quantitative evidence, to offer factual information. The form of presentation severely constrains possibilities at Level 5—alternative interpretations of what the text means. Because readers do not have access to much of Kay's life story, there are severe constraints on alternative readings of the data.

I raise the difficult issues about representation in Ginsburg's text because narrative analysts must consider them. Ginsburg, of course, does not come from the narrative tradition and is not interested in the constitutive aspects of language. I began with her example here because it is accessible and an important, if controversial, piece of feminist analysis (see Bennett, 1989). Ginsburg's theoretical conclusions are compelling, and I applaud how she brought the work back to her subjects (I return to these strengths when discussing validation in the conclusion). The book is more than Kay's story. But in my view, more could have been learned; Ginsburg simply did not push the narrative analysis far enough.

Future investigators could develop and extend the approach. A distinct advantage is Ginsburg's inclusion and interpretation across a number of cases: She generalized about the place of reproductive experience in the life stories of contrasting groups of women. Analysis of plot structures across interviews is a promising approach and could be adapted by others to study diversity among individuals who have had other life experiences. Diversity is displayed not so much by the contrasting themes different individuals chose to emphasize (as is the case in other forms of qualitative analysis) but by the contrasting ways individuals choose to put their accounts together, that is, the form of telling. For Ginsburg, form means both the substance of the turning points and the way they are sequenced into the life story. Others could extend the interpretive framework and "unpack" discourse further.

Some scholars in the life story tradition do attend to form and language. Working with archival oral histories, Yans-McLaughlin (1990) developed four areas to distinguish and code the narratives of Italian and Jewish immigrants who labored in New York City between 1900 and 1930: (a) how the speaker organized past, present and future time in the interview; (b) the way the speaker described him- or herself in relation to the past; (c) the way the speaker described, or failed to describe, interaction with objects and persons; and (d) the interaction of two sets of scripts, the analyst's and the speaker's. Each area involves detailed attention to language. In the second, for example, Yans-McLaughlin compared active and passive verb constructions about the self in history: "This happened to me" carries a world of difference in meaning compared to "I did this." The varied meanings of the same object—unionization struggles—also distinguished subjects.[19]

There is increasing interest, particularly among feminist researchers, in life history approaches (Geiger, 1986; Gluck & Patai, 1991; Reinharz,

1992). The challenge is to find ways of working with texts so the original narrator is not effaced, so she does not lose control over her words.

Linked Stories and Meaning in Conversation

Sociologist Bell (1988) studied the narratives of DES daughters to see how they understand and respond to risk and how some transform their experiences and become politically active. The place of DES (diethylstilbestrol) in the history of women's health is legendary. From 1940 to 1971, the drug was prescribed to prevent miscarriage, and between 500,000 and 3 million U.S. women were exposed prenatally. Their daughters are now vulnerable to a variety of reproductive tract problems, including infertility, miscarriages, and vaginal and cervical cancer. Paradoxically, DES daughters "must return to medicine—the very source of their problems— for information and treatment" (Bell, 1988, p. 99). In their interactions with medical institutions, they must cope continuously with risk and uncertainty because the full extent of the consequences of DES exposure are still unknown and because medical protocols for screening and management are changing.

Some daughters get politicized and join DES Action, an organization that grew out of the women's health movement. Bell, like Ginsburg, is interested in how activism happens, the connections between personal biography and public action.

NARRATIVE METHOD

Bell's (1988) approach was to ask open-ended questions, "listen with a minimum of interruptions, and tie my questions and comments to the DES daughters' responses by repeating their words . . . whenever possible" (p. 100). During the interview, women made sense of their experiences together with the listener by narration, telling stories that often linked at different points in the interview. Bell revealed a logic that links the stories, how when analyzed together the stories show individuals changing their consciousness about a health problem and becoming politicized. She also showed how meaning is produced through the interaction of two speakers.

Sarah, a middle-class woman in her early 30s, tells three stories over the course of a 1½-hour interview about how she came to know she was a DES daughter and how she transformed her knowledge into political action. The stories, which at first appear to be discrete and unconnected,

Abstract
002   L: how you found out you were a DES daughter,
003   and what it was like

Orientation
006   N: when I was around 19,
008   I was in college

Complicating action
009   and I went, to a, a gynecologist to get birth control
011   he was, he knew that I was a DES daughter because I had adenosis (1) um,
012   so he, told y'know he told me (2.5)
016   I think shortly after that,
017   (my mother) told me,
018   um and I either said "I know already" or, (inhale)

Resolution/coda
022   and I was so concerned at the time about getting birth control,
023   that I think it sort of didn't, um
024   it never really, became the major part of my life
025   it sort of f'flitted in and out (tch) (1.5)

Transcript 2.2. Story 1: "it sort of f'flitted in and out"

SOURCE: Bell (1988). Reprinted with permission by Ablex Publishing Corp.

connect a period of about 12 years in Sarah's life. Taken together, they depict a transformation in identity: "how Sarah has changed: from a passive patient to an active one, from an isolated individual to a participant in a woman's health organization" (Bell, 1988, p. 109).

In Story 1 (Transcript 2.2), Bell presented the core narrative of the first story, a radical reduction of a response to a skeleton plot (Mishler, 1986b). Here Sarah tells about when she first learned she was a DES daughter (she went for birth control in college) and what the knowledge meant (it was unremarkable). Labov's (1972) method of transcription and his structural categories are used to construct the text: Utterances are parsed into clauses, lines are numbered, and the parts of the narrative are identified by their function (to orient, carry the action, resolve it, etc.). To maintain focus on the core narrative, other parts of the discourse have been deleted (descriptions, asides, interactions between teller and listener, and most of the evaluation), although these are attended to at a later point in Bell's analysis. Other features of speech are preserved in the representation of the narrative, for example, the narrator's pauses (short ones are indicated by a comma, longer ones by their numbers in seconds in parentheses). For

---

Abstract

202	I then had some problems around, pregnancy,
203	that sort of brought the whole issue of DES (1.5) t'much more t'the forefront of my mind
204	and has made me much more, actively concerned about it,

Orientation

207	but, ah I, my first pregnancy, um, I had problems, due to DES

Complicating action

208	I got pregnant
224	and in the, middle of the night one night
225	my membranes broke,
226	and (1.2) y'know Mark r'rushed me to the hospital
227	and I delivered a baby girl,
228	(tch) who lived about eight hours
229	but she died
232	and even then, when the, resident the (1.5) (tch) doctor who was taking care of me
234	um, said, in the aftermath that maybe she thought it was due to DES,
235	um, I didn't believe her (1)
261	and then I went back
265	um she re- she had really done a lot of research
266	and sort of, presented me with a whole, scheme of how this could have happened
267	and why she thought it was related to the DES
270	then it was clear that it probably was,

Resolution/coda:

277	um (1) and that's when I (1.2) um began to accept the fact (1.2)
278	y'know once it made sense,

Transcript 2.3. Story 2: "and that's when I um began to accept the fact"

SOURCE: Bell (1988). Reprinted with permission by Ablex Publishing Corp.

Bell's interpretive purposes, this level of detail is absolutely necessary. Unlike Ginsburg, she is interested not only in the content of the narrative and plot line but how the story is told in another sense—the structures and language narrators chose in collaboration with a listener to represent the experience of change in political consciousness.

Attention to details of the discourse shows how Sarah's first and second stories are linked. The second story (see Transcript 2.3), told about 15 minutes after the first, tells how Sarah became actively concerned about DES after a miscarriage. She is no longer an adolescent exploring her sexuality but a married woman trying to have a baby. The meaning of the earlier diagnosis changes in this second context, as does the manner in

Abstract

301	L:	how did you, come to get involved with DES Action

Complicating action

302	N:	(3.5) (tch) (inhale) heard an ad on t.v. or the radio (1.5)
305		and I think I it if they had the tape number
306		and I called up
307		and asked for information
308		and they sent me their little packet
309		and I, joined
311		and then a while later
312		they sent me a card,
313		um that they were having coffee one of the the one of those like the one that you went to,
314		um and I couldn't go to that
322		um, but then I sort of felt like I had made an obligation to meet these people

Resolution

323	and, so I went ahead and met them you know
324	and liked them
325	and thought I it was someing [sic] something that I wanted to be more involved in

Coda

327	(1.5) and have stayed that way

Transcript 2.4. Story 3: "I no longer can be, blithe about it, and say not me"

SOURCE: Bell (1988). Reprinted with permission by Ablex Publishing Corp.

which she is told, by a woman physician, and Sarah begins to take her identity as a DES daughter seriously. The language of the second narrative shows a shift in consciousness, and the logic connecting the two moments in Sarah's life is evident in contrasts, as Bell (1988, p.112) displayed:

	Story 1		*Story 2*
038	out of my *mind*	203	t'the forefront of my *mind*
038	put *actively* put it out	204	more *actively* concerned
022	I was so *concerned* at the time about getting birth control	204	*concerned* about [the whole issue of DES]

Sarah's repetition of words makes each story more powerful, when viewed alongside the other, and shows how context and Sarah's response to it have altered. Without Bell's method of transcription and close attention to word choice, we would not see the evidence for transformation in consciousness.

In a third story that emerges toward the end of the interview (see Transcript 2.4), Sarah tells how she joined DES Action and became actively involved. The core narrative is sparse and factual, recounting Sarah's interactions with DES Action. She has moved from being "actively concerned" about her exposure to DES (Story 2) to acknowledging others exposed to DES and joining an organization built on this commonality between women (Story 3).

> Taken together, the three stories show how this DES daughter has coped with and responded to her exposure to DES. She explains how circumstances have changed, how her perceptions of events have changed, how her coping has changed, and how these changes are related to each other and to her evolving status as a political woman. (Bell, 1988, pp. 103-104)

To resolve puzzles in the three stories, Bell must go beyond the core narratives, which exclude the evaluation. For example, we know from Story 2 that Sarah came to "accept the fact" that she was a DES daughter, but what did it mean to her? What were the emotions that accompanied the shift in consciousness? Sarah, like all narrators, conveys meaning with asides that modify, by repeating words or phrases, by expressive sounds and silences. The reduction to a core narrative, although useful at the first analytic stage, excludes important features that are essential to a fuller interpretation.

Bell examined the long and complex texts, the full versions of the three stories, to see how Sarah moves away from a narrow view of DES to an understanding of her health in a social and emotional context. Drawing on the work of Mishler (1984) with medical interviews, she analyzed the dialogue between the voice of medicine and the voice of the life world in Sarah's account. Both voices are present throughout, but the relative power of each changes over the course of the three stories, and this change contributes to and reflects Sarah's politicization. The voice of medicine is present in the first and second stories in obvious ways: The doctor in the first story "knew I was a DES daughter because I had adenosis," and the doctor in the second story "presented me with a whole, scheme of how this could have happened . . . why she thought it was due to DES." The voice of the life world, and the complex emotions that came with knowing, emerge in an aside to Story 2 about the miscarriage:

248 I can remember when my mother said "Maybe this is due to the DES"
249 I said, "now don't be ridiculous,"
250 L: mhm
251 um because I did
252 I mean she was feeling awful
253 L: mhm
254 She was really d-
255 I mean we were all distraught
256 but y'know, to have her think that she had something to do with my losing the baby
257 was more than I could tolerate,

In the aftermath of the miscarriage, neither her doctor nor her mother could persuade Sarah that the tragedy was due to DES. Neither could penetrate the anguish. Sarah could not allow herself to know, so soon after losing the baby. A few weeks later in another conversation with the doctor who had done "a lot of research," she was presented with "a whole scheme of how this could have happened. . . . [I]t made sense."

The full version of the third story shows how, over time, Sarah has incorporated the voice of medicine into her life world, but also how she is resisting some of its limitations. An oppositional consciousness emerges. Sarah's logic has expanded: "Medicine had prescribed DES to her mother. Medicine has caused her miscarriage (by exposing her to DES and failing to warn her of reproductive risk associated with this exposure). Thus, medical logic is fallible" (Bell, 1988, p. 116). Sarah shifts the blame for her miscarriage to medicine in the evaluation of the third story:

329 (inhale), well, the more I had ti- the more removed I got from what had happened to me
330 and the longer it, the more time went by then the angrier I got about, some of the things that happened to me,
331 um, and the, I really felt like (4)
332 the fact that I that' that I shouldn't have lost that first baby
333 and that something different should have been done (1.5) (p. 116)

There is ambiguity here, as Bell discussed. Does line 332 refer to Sarah's own sense of responsibility for the miscarriage (she had put DES "out of [her] mind"), or does it refer to the fact that DES was prescribed to her mother? The line could also refer to another error—her doctor should have known that she was at risk of miscarriage and protected her. But "something different should have been done," and she is now involved in a social action organization that does just that, for all DES daughters.

In sum, Bell offers one model of narrative analysis that, in this case, clarifies identity transformation. By studying the sequence of stories in an interview, and the thematic and linguistic connections between them, an investigator can see how individuals tie together significant events and important relationships in their lives. The analyst identifies narrative segments, reduces stories to a core, examines how word choice, structure, and clauses echo one another, and examines how the sequence of action in one story builds on a prior one. Importantly, the emphasis is on language—how people say what they do and who they are—and the narrative structures they employ to construct experience by telling about it. The approach brings into view the interpersonal context: the connections between teller and listener that are the bedrock of all human interaction, including research interviews.

QUESTIONS

First, how did Bell transform talk into written form and how are narrative segments determined? She gave us two kinds of texts, the core of the three stories (as she has constructed them) and a "fuller" account that includes asides, evaluation, and the conversation in which the core narratives are embedded. Some might say the "fuller" texts are too full; they are difficult to read, especially if one is used to "cleaned" speech (the kind Ginsburg and most qualitative analysts present). Bell's texts certainly make more demands on the reader than Ginsburg's do; they require attention to disfluencies, pauses, breath intakes, lexical sounds (mhm, etc.), and interaction. Viewed from Scheff's (1990) microsociological frame, Bell gave prominence to the conversation that creates and sustains social bonds, in this case between women in a research interview. Such a focus requires minute attention to not only what is said but how it is said. Silences, for example, offer occasions for the other to speak. Her text displays the typically invisible process of how two women understand one another.

As is expected in this kind of analysis, Bell (1988) specified in a lengthy footnote her transcription conventions, how spoken language was transformed into written discourse—the transcribing process in Figure 1.1. She acknowledged that her transcripts "are not fully equivalent to the talk" (p. 103). They certainly exclude the gestures, gaze, and other nonverbal aspects of communication that carry meaning in conversation.

Second, what aspects of narrative serve as the basis for interpretations? Obviously, Bell attended to the narrative segments in the stream of talk of the interviews, specifically three, and the linguistic connections between them. She attended to sequence both within and across the stories. We are not told about other narratives in the interview and what their topics are, nor are we told much about the nonnarrative discourse. Bell's purpose was to show how Sarah used her DES experience to become a political woman, and the three narratives serve this focus.

Bell used "narrative" synonymously with "story," which she defined structurally. Narrative theory, as reviewed earlier, posits important distinctions: "Narrative" is an encompassing term of rhetoric, whereas "story" is a limited genre. Bell's method of analysis preserves the sequential organization her informant chooses, in collaboration with the listener, to recapitulate experience. Each story has a recognizable beginning and end (coda) and "consists of linked categories (episodes), connected to each other temporally and/or causally" (Bell, 1988, p. 101). Labov's structural framework (orientation, complicating action, evaluation, resolution) is essential to Bell's interpretive method.

There is also a relational component, not emphasized by Labov, namely, the reciprocal actions of teller and listener in beginning and ending a story and the listener's needs to encode and interpret it. Insight about the collaborative nature of story telling (see Paget, 1983) shaped how Bell represented the interview; the listener/questioner's utterances are included and analyzed. In fact, the listener supplies the abstract for the core narrative in Story 1 (see Transcript 2.2, lines 002-003), an unusual analytic step but one that fits with Bell's position on the interactional production of stories. One way to read Bell's text is as an analysis of the process of attunement in social interaction (Scheff, 1990), how through language mutual understanding and connection are accomplished, cognitively and emotionally, between women. The shape of Sarah's story, with clear orientation and building action followed by resolution, is related to Bell's role as attentive listener. She questioned, listened, and responded to what Sarah said and, in turn, Sarah clarified and developed her account. A different type of interaction might have produced a different story.

Bell did not discuss how she interpreted the boundaries of the stories, that is, defined beginnings and endings. (As noted earlier, this is by no means straightforward in every case and can be an important interpretive decision.) She did attend to language, scrutinizing certain words and clauses (e.g., "I shouldn't have lost that first baby"). By opening up different readings of words, she revealed the indeterminacy of language—how it is a system of signs that renders meaning ambiguous.

Finally, who determines what the narrative means and are alternative readings possible? In a very real sense meaning is collaboratively accomplished, involving teller, listener/analyst, and reader. The original speakers' words are not effaced; they are present in all their ambiguity and messiness. The analyst controls meaning to the extent that she selects what features of the discourse between the women will be the subject of her text, and she interprets the discourse. Bell decided what each of the three stories is about, but even here the teller is given a voice: The title of each of the three stories comes from Sarah's words. Determining the point of a narrative is an interpretive issue (Mishler, 1986b), but it can be done with more or less attention to the language of the subject, who may or may not make the point of her narrative explicit. The reader can see how the interpretations were derived and can imagine alternative ones (the fifth level of representation in Figure 1.1).

As a reader, I found myself questioning Bell's interpretation of Story 3 as a move to political action. I wondered how political Sarah really is. What, for example, is she doing because of her experience as a DES daughter to change the medical care system for women? Story 3 is flat, lacks elaboration and emotionality, and is occupied with concrete detail about how Sarah joined DES Action—hearing the ad, calling up, receiving the packet and card, meeting the women at a coffee. The process sounds more social than political. True, once the commonality with other women is discovered, organizing can begin (Ruzek, 1979). And the passage that immediately follows the core narrative (lines 329-333) says she's angry at the "things that happened to me." But it still was not clear to me that Sarah had shifted blame, collectivized her understanding of her situation, and taken political action. To resolve the interpretive issues, I examined the full text of Story 3 (Bell makes these available upon request to the reader) and found the following passage, separated from the lines about individual anger by a long pause, suggesting a transition in thought process:

335   (2.5) and if there was something that I could do to either help DES daughters be more assertive
336   and get better medical care (1.5) right away,
337   or, help, obstetricians, be more aware . . .
338   that that I wanted to do that

A bit later she talks about how "DES women are patronized," how "there are women out there who don't know that this is a problem." My interpretive questions were partially answered; I now tend to agree with Bell's reading of the story, although another reader might not see Sarah as political. But I am still puzzled by the flatness of Story 3 and wonder about the interview context that preceded it. A reader can enter into the meaning-making process (Level 5) only when the full narrative is included, or made available from the author.

Generalizing from the example, one application of Bell's analytic strategy is to reduce interview responses to core narratives and compare these across a sample. Narratives, especially those about important life experiences, are typically long, full of asides, comments, flashbacks, flashforwards, orientation, and evaluation. It is naive to think one can "just present the story" without some systematic method of reduction. The core narrative, a kind of radical surgery, is a way of rendering the "whole story" into a form that allows for comparison. (In Chapter 3, I provide further guidance about how to do narrative reduction.) Material that is excluded from the core, such as evaluation, can then be reintroduced, as Bell did, to interpret the variation in meaning of apparently similar plots. An investigator could combine Bell's textual approach with Ginsburg's plot/story distinction.

Poetic Structures and Meaning

The last example is drawn from my own work. *Divorce Talk* (Riessman, 1990a) examined how a sample of divorcing individuals make sense of their marriages and themselves and how the process is accomplished differently by women and men. Divorce brings in its stead considerable emotional difficulty for both genders and distinctive health problems for each. I wanted to see how emotional difficulties were voiced, and thus constructed, differently by women and men. I compared the talk about distress of each gender group and looked at the relationship between these results and a traditional quantitative analysis of depression for the sample. The two methods yielded very different findings and showed that women and men have distinctive vocabularies of emotion that have not been sufficiently acknowledged in mainstream mental health research.

NARRATIVE METHOD

I examined in some detail the talk of six members of my sample ($N = 105$), including Cindy (a pseudonym), portions of whose narrative are represented in Transcript 2.5. A young single parent on welfare, she had a depression score on the quantitative measure that was near the top of the range for women. As she put it, "Things are very very hard." She described four aspects of her life that were causing her difficulty, and these very nearly mirror the four role strains that predict depression for the entire sample of women in the quantitative analysis: children, money, worry about support payments, and lack of help (see Riessman, 1990a).

The form of Cindy's narrative intrigued me. I did not interview her, my coinvestigator did, and she departed from the structured set of questions after administering the depression scale (perhaps because of the many symptoms noted) and asked about "things that had been hard" lately. Cindy spoke at length about the difficulties she was facing and the emotions she was experiencing. The response "felt" like a narrative when I attempted to code it. I found myself not wanting to fragment it into discrete thematic categories but to treat it instead as a unit of discourse; it "sounded" like a narrative when I went to retranscribe it into a form suitable for that kind of analysis. It seemed to be structurally and thematically coherent and tightly sequenced. But it did not meet Labov's (1972, 1982) criteria: There was no plot in the traditional sense, few narrative clauses, and verbs were often in the present tense, not the simple past. These puzzles prompted me to search for other models for representing the discourse, other ways of understanding how Cindy organized her narrative and how she achieved coherence, so as to better grasp its meaning.

Transcript 2.5 displays my structural analysis of Cindy's narrative, informed in part by the work of James Gee (1985, 1986, 1991) on the poetic features of language. This is an ideal realization of the text, because it excludes interactions between teller and listener, false starts, pauses, discourse markers, nonlexical expressions, and other features of spoken language. (For the full narrative, see Riessman, 1990a, pp. 131-134.)

Cindy frames the narrative with a metaphor that binds the beginning of the narrative inextricably to its conclusion. She begins by likening her state of mind to walking, with a cloud over her, unable to see clearly through it. She refers to her unsettled emotions with this same image again, 10 minutes later in the interview, at the end of her long account ("I'm walking around waiting to decide"). The metaphor lends structural coherence to the narrative and suggests how it is bounded, that is, where it begins and ends. Thematically, the metaphor suggests motion and lack of resolution. Cindy has not arrived on some firm emotional ground.

In my representation, Cindy's speech (probably like all speech, linguists argue) has a stanza form, which lends coherence to the narrative. Stanzas are a series of lines on a single topic that have a parallel structure and sound as if they go together by tending to be said at the same rate and with little hesitation between lines. Gee (1985, 1986, 1991) argued that stanzas are a universal unit in planning speech and that poetry, in fact, builds on what we each do all the time. Poetry "fossilizes" and ritualizes what is in everyday speech. In Cindy's case, she gives in stanzas 3-6 a four-part explanation for why she feels so burdened, an explanation that she later expands in the narrative. As she lists the four areas that in her mind are causing her such difficulty—money, school, child care, and no time for herself—she moves from the outside in, from the most macro to the most micro issues. The tight stanza structure articulates a sense of constraint; the roles of provider, student, and mother create conflict because the expectations of each are so discordant, creating insoluble emotional dilemmas. In moving from the social to the personal, the sequence of the stanzas also suggests that Cindy has turned the responsibility for change from the outside inward. She feels the dilemma is hers to resolve, personally and privately, despite the fact that the sources of her distress are social.

Having outlined her four problems in four stanzas, Cindy develops each theme, amplifying in sequential order each of the causes of her distress. In the first part she explores the problem of money. She describes her struggle to support herself and explicitly locates the cause of the problem in the social environment (i.e., "a lot of it has to do with the welfare system changing"). She tells a narrative to explain "what happened," reconstructing and reinterpreting how state budget cuts, changing welfare policies, workfare, and the uncertainties of her job have made her financial situation "completely unstable."

At the time of the interview, Cindy is experiencing the effects of the first of the Reagan budget cuts in welfare expenditures and the beginnings of a new workfare program, which requires that she register for job training as soon as her child turns 6 (he was 5½). Because she is in a 4-year baccalaureate program (not considered "training" by the welfare department in her state), she stands a good chance of being "forced out of school," with only one year to go before graduating and, presumably, becoming more employable. Caught in the irrationality of these policies, Cindy decides to quit welfare. As a consequence, she must rely on child support payments from her former spouse that, she tells us elsewhere in the interview, are irregular and thus a source of worry.

Frame		
03	I've been walking around	
04	in this for the last month or so	
05	feeling that things are very very hard	
06	like I have a cloud over me and I'm very *confused*	

Affect and conflict		
09	I feel like	Stanza 1
10	I am too burdened	
11	and I can't imagine how	
12	to be less burdened	
13	I feel like	Stanza 2
14	I *need* to be doing everything I'm doing	
15	and so I don't know how to	
16	take some of the burden	
17	off of myself	
19	Well I need to work	Stanza 3
20	in order to earn a living	(money)
21	I need to	Stanza 4
23	go to school	(school)
23	so that I won't always have to work for nothing	
24	I need to	Stanza 5
25	be a good mother	(care of children)
26	'cause that's very important to me	
27	And I'd like to	Stanza 6
28	find a little free time	(time for self)
29	if I can	

Part 1: Money (narrative)	
33	alot of it has to do with the welfare system changing
35	Well I used to be on welfare
37	. . . they cut me a whole lot
38	because I work also
48	but so my choice at that point was
49	either to go off completely
50	and get money from him
51	or quit working
52	and I
53	at that point it sounded like a good idea
54	to quit work
55	so that I could
56	go to school and not feel
57	like I had so many things to do
58	but um financially I just couldn't do it

Transcript 2.5. Cindy's Narrative

SOURCE: Adapted from Riessman (1990a). Reprinted by permission from Rutgers University Press and the author.

59	there was no way I could do it.	
60	And also with workfare looming ahead	
61	I was worried that I'd get	
62	forced out of school	
63	and I only have like a year to go	
64	so because I didn't want to take a chance	
65	of being forced out of school	
66	I just quit welfare.	
75	I don't know how long my job is going to hold out	
78	So my financial situation is just	
79	completely unstable at this point.	

Part 2: School

80	And I ended up taking two incompletes	Stanza 7
81	out of three classes I was taking in school.	

Summary

82	So it's making me think that	Stanza 8
83	trying to go to school	
84	*and* work and be a good mother is too much	
85	but I don't know how I can not do it.	

Part 3: Care of children

86	And at the same time for some reason	Stanza 9
87	my son's going through a really clingy spell again	
88	And he probably does it right when I can least	
89	afford to deal with it you know.	

Summary

90	So it's just a lot of stuff all at once	Stanza 10
91	in the last month or so.	

Part 4: Self (narrative)

92	and so I've been
93	with all this other stuff I've been
94	actually needy myself
95	you know wanting
96	wanting someone to come home to
97	who would say "Hey sit down
98	I'll fix you a drink
99	let's chit chat about the day"
100	you know someone to nurture *me*.
101	And so I've been more aware of not having that person

Frame (return to affect and conflict)

102	I feel like	Stanza 11
103	I have to make a decision	
105	I don't know what to decide so	
106	I'm walking around waiting to decide.	

Cindy leaves the narrative mode after summarizing the first part in lines 78-79. She does not tell another formal narrative again until later but instead uses nonnarrative forms in the middle two parts (Parts 2 and 3 of Transcript 2.5) to explain the sources of her distress and the emotional conflicts they create in her. The second part—about the strain associated with school—merely reports in a couplet, succinctly and tersely, how she resolved the dilemma of role overload. Like her earlier statement about financial strain ("I just quit welfare"), the active voice here says how she resolved her dilemmas ("I ended up taking two incompletes"). As if to summarize, she then explicitly restates the theme of being burdened in a 4-line stanza in lines 82-85. The stanza captures the essence of the bind that welfare policies have created for Cindy: Holding a job is necessary because of welfare cuts and workfare, but going to school is necessary to get a decent job.

In the third part, Cindy elaborates on her problems being a good parent— her 5-year-old son is "going through a really clingy spell again." He's doing this at a time when she can "least afford to deal with it." The irony in her choice of the word "afford" is apparent: Her emotional resources for parenting are as limited as are her financial ones.

In the summarizing couplet of lines 90-91, Cindy makes a statement that ties the three parts together. The recent past has been especially difficult, she says, because of the combination of money, school, and child-care demands ("a lot of stuff all at once"). It is the piling up of role strains that makes her feel burdened, not any single problem.

The fourth part, lines 92-101, picks up on a theme Cindy put forward earlier (no time for herself) but gives it a twist. In the context of "all this other stuff," she's been feeling "actually needy" herself. It is not time alone that she wants as much as somebody to support and nurture her.

The focus of the fourth part is not on events that have happened but events she wishes would happen, and consequently Cindy tells a hypothetical narrative. Through dialogue, she creates a text within a text, a multivoiced narrative (Wolf & Hicks, 1989) with texture and dimensionality that is emotionally affecting both because of what she says and how she says it. To convey the fantasy, she constructs a hypothetical conversation in lines 96-101. Like her son, she wants someone to hold on to.

Cindy concludes the narrative but does not resolve the dilemmas it sets forth. Unlike many narratives about events that have happened in the past, this one, concerning role strains and distress, lacks firm resolution and closure because the narrator is still in the middle of the conflict. She

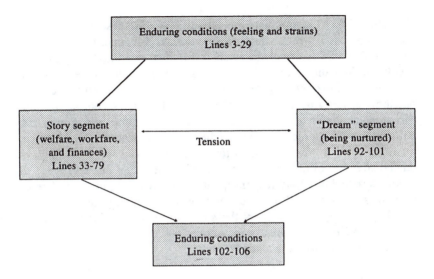

Figure 2.1.

returns in lines 102-106 to the metaphor of walking, the present tense, the phrase ("I feel like") and the stanza structure with which she began the narrative many minutes before. She is preoccupied with making a decision (she mentions this three times in four lines), but exactly what decision is ambiguous. What is clear is that Cindy feels overwhelmed in the face of multiple pressures with no one to help. Although at one level the origins of her problems are distinctly public, her experience of them is personal and private. As she assesses her situation, it will be "resolved" by some decision *she* has yet to make. No political movement is present in Cindy's account, as in Kay's and Sarah's, that could provide alternative understandings and collective solutions.

Figure 2.1 represents a schematic of the essential tension, as I see it, in the structure of the discourse. Lines 3-29 and lines 102-106 speak of enduring conditions that form the context for two narrative segments. Enduring portions of the discourse are not narrative; they last and have an ongoing quality that testifies to the durative, the progressive, and the nonspecific. It is within these enduring states, which begin and end the discourse, that the two narrative segments are embedded, the first a story about a specific past event involving welfare and workfare (lines 33-79) and the second a hypothetical narrative about a dream of being nurtured (lines 92-101). Although there are parts in between, these two narratives are counterposed, which attests to an essential dilemma: the actual and the possible, the real and the wished-for. Just as Cindy's explanation pivots on thematic contrasts (welfare vs. school, child vs. self), so too does its form, juxtaposing the nonnarrative and the narrative, the story and the dream.[20] Like the previous two examples, this is a narrative about discordance: the breach in the ordinary, expected course of a human life, a theme that Cindy realizes through the tight organization of a narrative.

To summarize, my approach offers another model for analyzing extended stretches of talk in research interviews that feel like narratives. It involves reducing a long response, parsing it according to a set of rules into lines, stanzas, and parts, examining its organizing metaphors, and creating a schematic to display the structure—a very different form of analysis than in the previous two examples.[21] (Chapter 3 gives more detail on how the reduction was made.)

QUESTIONS

Because this is my work, I find it more difficult than with the previous two examples to critically examine it, but let me try. First, how has talk been transformed into a written text, and how are narrative segments determined? Cindy's long response is reduced, not to a core narrative or skeleton plot—which would leave practically nothing—but with reference to Gee's (1985, 1986, 1991) theory of the units of speech. He draws on oral rather than written, text-based models of language and emphasizes prosodic and paralinguistic aspects, such as changes in pitch and intonation. To discern patterning, I attend to how the narrative is said, that is, the organization of the discourse system into lines, stanzas, and parts. The representation of talk and mode of analysis could be accused of formalism (for a response to this criticism see Gee, 1991, pp. 15-16), and one potential publisher called my approach "pretentious."

When I began working on Cindy's long response with Gee's theory of discourse units, I was initially skeptical. I wondered whether speech is, in fact, structured as he argues and still prefer to think of poetic structures as a way to represent discourse, not intrinsic to it. Whatever the philosophical differences, repeated listening to tapes sensitized me to subtleties of language that I never was aware of before, and certainly never attended to in previous transcripts—intonation contours, rising and falling pitch, pauses and discourse markers (well, and, so, nonlexical expressions like "uh") that, Gee argues, set off stanzas in a narrative. I found that each of the four parts of Cindy's narrative (see Transcript 2.5) is, in fact, set off with such a marker. As I became more familiar with the transcription conventions, I heard structure: the building blocks of the narrative, groups of lines said together about a single topic, a vignette, in the form of a stanza.

> Each stanza is a particular "take" on a character, action, event, claim, or piece of information, and each involves a shift of focal participants, focal events, or a change in the time or framing of events from the preceding stanza. Each stanza represents a particular perspective, not in the sense of who is doing the seeing, but in terms of what is seen; it represents an image, what the "camera" is focused on, a "scene." (Gee, 1991, pp. 23-24)

The transcript represents a reduction based on my hearing, with the earphones of Gee's theory on my head, of how Cindy said her reply to the question about "things that had been hard" lately. The form of representation draws attention to the transcribing/analyzing interface in Figure 1.1, namely, how decisions about displaying talk are inseparable from the process of interpretation.

Ironically, certain features of speech that are critical to analyzing the structure of the narrative are excluded from the representation of it (e.g., pauses and discourse markers). The interaction between teller and listener that produced the narrative is also not represented. There is no place for an emotional moment between the women as the narrative ends (immediately after the hypothetical narrative in Part 4, there is a long pause, broken by what sounds like sniffling, followed by joint laughing). It could even be argued that Gee's method strips the interview context from the narrative. (Because of this concern, I elected in *Divorce Talk* to present the full response and Transcript 2.5, a strategy that required some persuasion of my editor.)

What is the definition of narrative here? I use the term two ways: first, to describe Cindy's entire response, which meets general criteria (sequence, thematic, and structural coherence); and, second, to describe Parts 1 and 4 which meet more limited criteria (temporal order, evaluation). In Figure 2.1, I am departing from Gee's method but make a similar argument for a complex discourse form: embedded narrative segments within an overarching narrative that includes nonnarrative parts. Labov's (1972, 1982; Labov & Waletzky, 1967) theory and the relatively simple stories he analyzes do not provide an adequate model for subjective experiences, events that unfold over time and even extend into the present, as Cindy's narrative does. Hers is as much about affective "actions," things the narrator feels and says to herself, as it is about "what happened" in a more objective sense.[22]

Second, what aspects of the narrative constitute the basis for interpretation? Obviously not interaction, the focus of attention here is on linguistic choices Cindy makes and the patterning of her discourse, or how the text is spoken. Gee (1991) argued that many interpretations are ruled out by the structure of the spoken narrative. My interpretation takes account of structural properties (frames, stanzas, parts), key metaphors (walking), key words ("afford"), verb tense ("I got cut way down" vs. "I just quit welfare"), how substantive themes get developed through these, and other linguistic choices. I go beyond the text and make inferences about context, informed by my politics, notably changing welfare policies and their effect on the situation of single mothers in U.S. society.

By excluding the interaction between teller and listener that produced the narrative, I treat it as sole-authored, as "inside" the designated narrator. The situation of its telling is not part of the interpretation, that is, how the account takes a particular shape and meaning because of the interactional context. It could be argued, for example, that Cindy develops her narrative this way because both speakers agree on a topic, "things that have been hard lately." A different kind of interaction might have produced a different account. (For an extension of Gee's approach to discourse between speakers, see Mishler, 1992.)

Finally, who determines what the narrative means, and are alternative readings possible? Cindy's words and my interpretations are both available, although they are conflated by the way talk is represented (the case in all three examples). The basis for my interpretations, particularly about structure, is not visible in Transcript 2.5, only in the full response (portions of which are reproduced in Chapter 3). The teller has, if not the final word, at least the first word on which interpretation depends.

When I was analyzing Cindy's long narrative, I was led into my sense of it by its organization. She could have said what she had to say in several different ways. What did the form she chose signify? I claim that we can come close to seeing into her subjective experience—what life "means" to her at the moment of telling—through experiencing the tension in the structure of the narrative (the juxtaposition of the real and the wished for, the story and the dream).[23]

Notes

17. *Contested Lives* (Ginsburg, 1989a) has had a very mixed reaction from feminists. For a review which, among other things, criticizes the book for a lack of attention to race and class, see Bennett (1989). As I suggest in the fifth level of Figure 1.1, a life history has an afterlife: Audiences respond to the published work (Blackman, 1992).

18. Within the life history tradition, some scholars do include the interaction that produced a particular narrative in the analysis (see Anderson & Jack, 1991).

19. For an example of different understandings of the word *dependent* in a study of depressed women, see Jack (1991).

20. I thank Dennie Wolf for her insights about structural tension in Cindy's narrative and for Figure 2.1, which she drafted.

21. In *Divorce Talk*, I combined the approach with a statistical analysis of the entire sample (Riessman, 1990a). Close attention to Cindy's experience provided a context for interpreting a multiple-regression equation, for example. Lack of money became more than a variable that predicted depression: Emotional distress is produced in Cindy's case by social policies that force women to make choices, between job, school, and welfare eligibility, that compromise their efforts to become self-supporting and bring depression in their stead. Similarly, Cindy's experience with a clingy son and her longing for care herself show what other variables in the quantitative model—child care and lack of help—actually mean in context.

22. For more on Cindy's narrative against Labov's criteria, see Riessman (1990a, pp. 253-254).

23. Some might argue for a different interpretation. Although not working with Cindy's narrative but with one Gee (1991) presents, a very experienced student in my doctoral qualitative analysis class said its meaning was self-evident, that Gee's elaborate structural analysis was not needed to make sense of it. The text we were discussing was the long account of a woman suffering from schizophrenia, which Gee represents in lines, stanzas, and strophes that convincingly display coherence. The next week, as an exercise, I presented the class with a different representation of the same stretch of talk, transcribed the normal way, that is, in continuous lines. Most agreed that in this representation the woman's talk was incoherent, and the clinical psychology students were quick to read it as "loose," a "flight of ideas," prima facie evidence of schizophrenic thought process. The text had a different meaning. The exercise moved us all and convinced everyone (except perhaps the skeptical student) that, although texts can be open to several (but not infinite) readings, meaning and textual representation are dependent on one another.

54

3. DOING NARRATIVE ANALYSIS

How does an investigator do narrative work? A series of interpretive
decisions confront all investigators. Returning to Figure 1.1, investigators
must consider how to facilitate narrative telling in interviews (Level 2),
transcribe for the purposes at hand (Level 3), and approach narratives
analytically (Level 4). My thoughts on these issues are offered, not as a
set of prescriptions but as guidelines for getting started. There is no standard
set of procedures compared to some forms of qualitative analysis.

Telling

To encourage those we study to attend to and tell about important moments
in their lives, it is necessary to provide a facilitating context in the research
interview, which implicates the interview schedules we develop. Certain
kinds of open-ended questions are more likely than others to encourage
narrativization. Compare "when did X happen?," which asks for a discrete
piece of information, with "tell me what happened," which asks for a more
extended account of some past time. It is preferable to ask questions that
open up topics and allow respondents to construct answers, in collaboration with listeners, in the ways they find meaningful (Mishler, 1986a). But
even questions that could be answered by a yes or no can generate
extended accounts: Studying racism in the everyday lives of black women,
Essed (1988) asked, "Have you ever experienced discrimination when you
applied for a job?"; many women responded with stories.

To study violence, Labov (1982) asked inner-city youth, "Were you
ever in a situation where you thought you were in serious danger of getting
killed?" To study moral conflict among teachers/parents, Attanucci (1991)
asked, "Would you describe a time when you weren't sure what the right
thing to do was and you had to decide?" Because the impulse to narrate
is so natural, and apparently universal, it is almost inevitable that these
kinds of questions will produce narrative accounts, provided interviewing
practices do not get in the way.

Some investigators have developed visual aids to elicit narratives.
Veroff et al. (in press) gave the following instructions to the newlywed
couples they interviewed:

> Tell me in your own words the story of your relationship. I have no set questions
> to ask you. . . . I just want you to tell me about your lives together as if it
> were a story with a beginning, a middle and how things will look in the fu-

ture . . . there is no right or wrong way to tell your story . . . just tell me in any way that is most comfortable . . . it's something that couples really enjoy doing . . . each of you can talk, and I hope to hear from both of you . . . you can agree about the story; you can disagree . . . any way that seems comfortable for you.

To facilitate recall, the interviewer presents a storyboard to the couple and says:

To help you think of your story, this describes most people's storyline. You see that a storyline for a marriage usually includes each of these parts: how you met; how you got interested in one another; becoming a couple; planning to get married; the wedding itself; what life was like after the wedding; what married life is like right now; and what you think married life will be like in the future. . . . to get you started why don't each of you tell me what your life was like before the two of you met? . . . now let's hear the story of your relationship. How did it all begin? (pp. 11-12)

Interestingly, couples do not always follow instructions, they do not tell their stories in the linear form Veroff et al. (in press) are looking for.

My preference is for less structure in interview instruments, in the interest of giving greater control to respondents. I advise my students to develop an interview guide (Merton, Fiske, & Kendall, 1956/1990): 5 to 7 broad questions about the topic of inquiry, supplemented by probe questions in case the respondent has trouble getting started ("Can you tell me more about that?" "What was the experience like for you?"). Interviews are conversations in which both participants—teller and listener/questioner—develop meaning together, a stance requiring interview practices that give considerable freedom to both. Listeners can clarify uncertainties with follow-up questions and "the answers given continually inform the evolving conversation" (Paget, 1983, p. 78).

As someone who has done quantitative and qualitative analysis and attempted to join them in a single study (Riessman, 1990a), I advise students that open-ended questions designed to produce narrative accounts can be combined in the same interview with closed-ended items or self-administered questionnaires. Different data collection methods yield different information, and they have to be interpreted differently. Students typically have to meet academic departmental expectations for quantification, and the approach is better suited to collect certain kinds of data, such as demographic information. Students who combine methods will have to cross borders, risk being defined as illegal aliens, transgress the "hedgerows that define and protect traditional interests and practices" (Mishler, 1991a, p. 102).

Returning to research interviews, narratives often emerge when you least expect them. In studying divorcing women and men, for example, my coinvestigator and I adapted an item originally used by Goode (1956): "Would you state, in your own words, what was the main cause of your divorce" (p. 359). We expected the question to stimulate a list of marital problems, which we could code thematically, as Goode had, and compare the "themes of complaint" in marriages in the 1980s with those in the 1950s. In response to the question, however, many in our sample took the floor and told long stories about their marriages: how they began, what happened during the course, the moment that turned the tide, and so on. In these evolving accounts, an initial complaint often turned out not to be the reason the individual finally decided to leave. (I suspect Goode's sample tried to tell stories too.)

Provided investigators can give up control over the research process and approach interviews as conversations, almost any question can generate a narrative. Sociolinguists argue that events must be "reportable" to warrant a lengthy turn at talk in everyday conversation (Labov, 1982; Polanyi, 1985), but the opposite is also true; tellers can make events reportable in any interaction by making a story out of them. Presumably anything of an experiential nature is worthy of a lengthy account or at least can be made so.

Transcribing

"Crunching text requires text to first be put in crunchable form" (Van Maanen, 1988, p. 131). Taping and transcribing are absolutely essential to narrative analysis. Students invariably struggle with the issue of how to transcribe the tapes of interviews, which in qualitative interviews are often lengthy. Unfortunately, there is no easy answer here because transforming talk into written text, precisely because it is a representation, involves selection and reduction. My general advice is to begin with a rough transcription, a first draft of the entire interview that gets the words and other striking features of the conversation on paper (e.g., crying, laughing, very long pauses). Then go back and retranscribe selected portions for detailed analysis.

In settings where the telling of long stories is not expected, such as medical interviews, patients often have to fight for the floor to tell one. Mishler, Clark, Ingelfinger, and Simons (1989) and Clark and Mishler (1992) selected from rough transcriptions those segments for retranscription that best displayed the subtle process of negotiation between doctor and patient about the relevance of a personal narrative to the medical problem at hand. In one text, the physician fails to attend to the patient's story and she becomes visibly upset, whereas in another case a physician facilitates the development of a story that is essential to the diagnosis. Texts created in retranscription allowed for analysis of interruptions, pauses, and other spoken features of discourse that distinguished attentive patient care.

Investigators often delegate transcription to others, such as graduate students and secretaries. Scholars from a particular theoretical persuasion (e.g., ethnomethodology) often want more detailed transcriptions from the onset, and there are clerical workers who are accustomed to these requests and highly skilled in their ability to represent discourse on a two dimensional page. Most transcribers, however, will need considerable guidance about how precise to be.

An experience taught me about the issues firsthand. Early in the divorce study, when my coinvestigator went back to check the accuracy of the transcriptions, she discovered utterances on the tape that did not appear in the typescript. In response to our query, the transcriber said she left out asides, talk that "wasn't in answer to the question." Yet these seeming irrelevancies provided context essential to interpretation and, not infrequently, the asides were narratives, the heart of the matter. The edited transcriptions had to be redone.

I spend considerable time scrutinizing the rough drafts of transcriptions, often across a number of interviews, before going to the next level. It is here that analytic induction (Katz, 1983) is most useful. A focus for analysis often emerges, or becomes clearer, as I see what respondents say. Studies, like narrative accounts, are jointly produced; as investigators interact with subjects, analytic ideas change (Mishler, 1992). As I scrutinize transcripts, features of the discourse often "jump out," stimulated by prior theoretical interests and "fore-structures" of interpretation (Heidegger, 1927/1962).

I remember, for example, working with the transcript of an interview with a working-class Puerto Rican woman and noticing places where the middle-class Anglo interviewer misunderstood the sequence of the narrative. Because of a long-standing interest in class and cultural diversity, the interaction caught my attention. To locate more precisely the source of the failure in communication, I needed to relisten to the tape and produce a more detailed rendering of key moments in the conversation. Close textual analysis revealed contrasting assumptions about time between the women—whether a narrative should be organized temporally or topically, not present in interviews between Anglos, which I related to broader cultural themes (Riessman, 1987). Trouble in interaction provided a fruitful beginning point.

I know of no way to avoid the painstaking work of personally retranscribing the sections of text that appear to take a narrative form (which I put brackets around as I'm working with the rough drafts, most of which are nonnarrative, e.g., question and answer exchanges, arguments, chronicles, and other forms of discouse). In my experience, the task of identifying narrative segments and their representation cannot be delegated. It is not a technical operation but the stuff of analysis itself, the "unpacking" of structure that is essential to interpretation. By transcribing at this level, interpretive categories emerge, ambiguities in language are heard on the tape, and the oral record—the way the story is told— provides clues about meaning. Insights from these various sources shape the difficult decision about how to represent oral discourse as a written text.

Determining where a narrative begins and ends and the listener/questioner's place in producing it are textual as well as analytic issues. Listening for entrance and exit talk (Jefferson, 1979) often helps define relatively simple narratives. For example, a divorcing man I interviewed complained that his wife put the children before him, then said "And I'll clarify this with an example," to which I replied "O.K." We negotiated in this brief exchange an opening in the conversation for a narrative. He then told a long story, which I did not interrupt except to say "uh-huh" about a particular time where his wife refused to accompany him to a dog show (see Riessman, 1990a, pp. 103-104). The word "example" introduced the pasttime world of the story, and he made the same word choice many minutes later to signal an exit from the world; the incident was "a classic example of the whole relationship," and he returned from past to present time. Not all narratives are so clearly bounded. Remember Bell (1988) shows how the listener supplies the abstract for several of Sarah's stories (see Transcripts 2.2 and 2.4).

Once the boundaries of a narrative segment are chosen, I find it useful in retranscribing to parse the narrative into numbered lines. (Jefferson [1979],

Table 3.1.

Rough Transcription	Retranscription
This is actually a crucial incident because I finally got up and went into the other room. She was [talking to her lover on the phone] in the laundry room with the door closed. I knocked on the door and said, "When are you going to be done with this?" 'Cause we were going to talk. And she held her hand like this and went "No." And I got absolutely bullshit. I put my fist through the door, which is not the kind of stuff that I do, you know. I'm not a real physically violent person at all.	30 and (p) finally, ah it's, this is actually a crucial incident [A] 31 because I *finally* got up and (p) [CA] 32 and (p) went into the other room [CA] 33 (p) she was in the laundry room with the door closed and [O] 34 (p) knocked on the door and said [CA] 35 "When are you going to be done with this?" [CA] 36 'cause we, we were going to talk. [O] 37 And she kind of held up her hand like this and went "no." [CA] 38 And I got absolutely bullshit [E] 39 I put my *fist* through the door (I:uh-huh) [R] 40 which is not the kind of stuff that I, that I do, you know [E] 41 I'm *not* a real physically violent person at all. [E]

presented a widely used system of typescript notation; also see West [1984, pp. 42-44].) I use Labov's (1972, 1982) framework to see how simple narratives are organized, an essential first step to interpreting them. To review, well-formed stories, according to Labov, are made from a common set of elements and every clause has a function: to provide an abstract for what follows (A), orient the listener (O), carry the complicating action (CA), evaluate its meaning (E), and resolve the action (R). Table 3.1 shows on the left a rough transcription of a portion of a divorce narrative and, on the right, my retranscription of the same stretch of talk into clauses that correspond to Labov's functional elements (noted at the end of each line). Notice how the representation on the left excludes disfluencies and subtle features of the discourse present in the representation on the right, like short pauses (p), utterances of the interviewer (I: uh-huh), verbal emphasis, and word repetitions.

Many narratives do not lend themselves to Labov's framework, although the model often provides a useful starting point. Narratives are not a singular form of discourse, and cross-cultural studies suggest variation in story grammar (McCabe, 1991, in press; Michaels, 1981; Riessman, 1987). Labov makes strong claims from his limited materials for clear beginnings and endings to stories, but there are few rules for partitioning more complex stretches from interviews that feel like narrativizations. Boundaries may depend on the investigator's overall framework and vice versa: One can locate stories and other narrative segments in a stretch of talk and inductively build a framework. Informants direct interpretation by the way they organize their narratives, including parts and their relation to the whole.

Although parsing helps to closely examine a text, collaborators can differ in parsing the same text. Some variation should be expected "because hearers and readers hear and read differently from each other, and differently from what speakers and writers may intend" (Gee, 1991, p. 27). Figure 1.1 and my earlier discussion suggest how multilayered interpretation is.

Analyzing

Analysis cannot be easily distinguished from transcription. As Mishler (1991b) noted, "How we arrange and rearrange the [interview] text in light of our discoveries is a process of testing, clarifying and deepening our understanding of what is happening in the discourse" (p. 277). Close and repeated listenings, coupled with methodic transcribing, often leads to insights that in turn shape how we choose to represent an interview narrative in our text. As the research report is being prepared, there is also, of course, much more explicit reliance on preferred concepts and theories.

It is not always clear at the beginning of a research project what features of speech will prove to be essential.[24] I discourage students from tightly specifying a question that they will answer with data from narrative accounts because analytic induction, by definition, causes questions to change and new ones to emerge.

Two strategies for data reduction and interpretation were featured in Chapter 2: reduction to the core narrative used by Bell and the analysis of poetic structures used by me. Both examples involve a selection of key aspects of a longer narrative and, for those interested in adapting these approaches, it may help to show more precisely how reductions are made. (Ginsburg does not provide sufficient information to allow inclusion here.)

The left side of Table 3.2 displays a segment of the narrative, already retranscribed into lines, in which Sarah tells about her DES experience. On the right is Bell's (1988) reduction. The core narrative, which includes all of Labov's elements except evaluation, provides a skeleton plot, a generalizable structure that investigators could use to compare the plots of individuals who share a common life event.

Turning to my reduction of Cindy's account of her emotions and burden, Table 3.3 displays two representations of the first 29 lines. On the left is my retranscription into numbered lines, which are noticeably shorter than Bell's because I was guided by Gee's framework rather than Labov's. I listened for the speaker's changes in pitch to make line breaks rather than attending to the function of a clause in the narrative. Notice how my subsequent reduction of the narrative segment, on the right side of Table 3.3, excludes all the interviewer's utterances, as well as the teller's false starts, break-offs, and other features that obscure the poetic structures I am interested in. Others are extending Gee's approach to analyze interaction (Mishler, 1992).

To avoid the tendency to read a narrative simply for content, and the equally dangerous tendency to read it as evidence for a prior theory, I recommend beginning with the structure of the narrative: How is it organized? Why does an informant develop her tale *this* way in conversation with *this* listener? To the fullest extent possible, I start from the inside, from the meanings encoded in the form of the talk, and expand outward, identifying, for example, underlying propositions that make the talk sensible, including what is taken for granted by speaker and listener. The strategy privileges the teller's experience, but interpretation cannot be avoided. Individuals' narratives are situated in particular interactions but also in social, cultural, and institutional discourses, which must be brought to bear to interpret them. Nor can investigators bypass difficult issues of power: Whose voice is represented in the final product? How open is the text to other readings? How are we situated in the personal narratives we collect and analyze? It is essential, in my view, to open up these interpretive issues for readers to see.

Ultimately, of course, the features of an informant's narrative account an investigator chooses to write about are linked to the evolving research question, theoretical/epistemological positions the investigator values, and, more often than not, her personal biography. If this circularity makes some readers uncomfortable, I can only offer the comfort of a long tradition of interpretive and hermeneutic inquiry. Close analysis of narrative derives legitimation from this tradition and also extends it in new ways.

Table 3.2.

Retranscribed Version of Story 1	*Core Narrative of Story 1*
001 L: uh (1) the way I've usually started these is to ask	Abstract
002 how you found out you were a DES daughter,	002 L: how you found out you were a DES daughter
003 and what it was like	003 and what it was like
004 N: (1) um, it's funny because the, details are fuzzy, in my head	Orientation
005 what I, think happened, was um (1) (tch)	006 N: when I was around 19,
006 when I was around 19,	008 I was in college
007 I we-	
008 I was in college	Complicating action
009 and I went, to a, a gynecologist to get birth control	009 and I went, to a, a gynecologist to get birth control
010 and, I happened to be lucky with my first exam	011 he was, he knew that I was a DES daughter because I had adenosis (1) um,
011 he was, he knew that I was a DES daughter because I had adenosis (1) um,	012 so he, told y'know he told me (2.5)
012 so he, told y'know he told me (2.5)	016 I think shortly after that,
013 and I don't remember how it became (laughs) clear between my mother and I,	017 [my mother] told me,
014 that (1.5) that uh 'cause she didn't know I was going to the gynecologist	018 um and I either said "I know already" or, (inhale)
015 that she (1)	
016 I think shortly after that,	Resolution/coda
017 she told me	022 and I was so concerned at the time about getting birth control,
018 um and I either said "I know already" or, (inhale)	023 that I think it sort of didn't, um,
019 um (1) but I didn't learn from her directly first	024 it never really, became the major part of my life
020 um I learned it from this doctor (1.5)	025 (tch) (1.5) it sort of f'flitted in and out
021 L: uhm	
022 N: and I was so concerned at the time about getting birth control,	
023 that I think it sort of didn't, um,	
024 it never really, became the major part of my life	
025 it sort of f'flitted in and out (tch)	

Table 3.3.

Retranscription	Analysis of Poetic Structures
01 About (p) things that are hard?	**FRAME**
02 Well um I don't know what's hard (laughs)	03 I've been walking around
03 I've been walking around	04 in this for the last month or so
04 in this for the last month or so	05 feeling that things are very very hard
05 feeling that things are very very hard	06 like I have a cloud over me and I'm very *confused*
06 like I have a cloud over me	**AFFECT AND CONFLICT**
07 and I'm very *confused*	**Stanza 1**
08 and I can't (P)	09 I feel like
09 I feel like	10 I am too burdened
10 I am too burdened	11 and I can't imagine how
11 and I can't imagine how	12 to be less burdened
12 to be less burdened	**Stanza 2**
13 I feel like	13 I feel like
14 I I *need* to be doing everything I'm doing	14 I *need* to be doing everything I'm doing
15 (P) and so I don't know how to	15 and so I don't know how to
16 take some of the burden	16 take some of the burden
17 off of myself (P)	17 off of myself
18 *Int.*: Why do you think you need to be doing everything?	**ENDURING ROLE STRAINS**
19 *Cindy*: (P) Well ah I I need to work	**Stanza 3 (money)**
20 in order to earn a living.	19 Well I need to work
21 (p) I need to ah	20 in order to earn a living
22 go to school	**Stanza 4 (school)**
23 so that I won't always have to work for nothing.	21 I need to
24 I need to	22 go to school
25 be a good mother	23 so that I won't always have to work for nothing
26 'cause that's very important to me.	**Stanza 5 (care of children)**
27 (P) And (P) I'd like to	24 I need to
28 find a little free time	25 be a good mother
29 if I can (laughs).	26 'cause that's very important to me
	Stanza 6 (time for self)
	27 And I'd like to
	28 find a little free time
	29 if I can

Note

24. So save tapes. I reused some in the early stages of the divorce study, which made retranscription of narratives from them impossible.

CONCLUSION

Two large issues remain: validation and the limits of narrative analysis. They represent as yet unresolved dilemmas for the field. I open up the topics here in the hope that future investigators will carry them forward.

Validation

How are we to evaluate a narrative analysis? Can one tell a better one from a worse one? Prevailing concepts of verification and procedures for establishing validity (from the experimental model) rely on realist assumptions and consequently are largely irrelevant to narrative studies. A personal narrative is not meant to be read as an exact record of what happened nor is it a mirror of a world "out there." Our readings of data are themselves located in discourses (e.g., scientific, feminist, and therapeutic).

Some might say the criteria of art are sufficient for appraising a "blurred genre" (Geertz, 1983): Does a narrative analysis move us? If narrative work is viewed as literary craft rather than a social scientific activity (Manning, 1987), art is sufficient. Although I welcome artistic representations (too much social science writing is formulaic and technically compulsive), there is need for something more, in my view. What that "more" might be is the topic of this chapter.

I present a few caveats and distinctions first. The historical truth[25] of an individual's account is not the primary issue. Narrativization assumes point of view. Facts are products of an interpretive process; "facts and interpretations require and shape one another" (Stivers, 1993, p. 421). Individuals construct very different narratives about the same event (Chafe, 1980); there are marked disparities between the ordering of telling and the ordering of occurrences in something as straightforward as a horse race (Goodman, 1980). It is always possible to narrate the same events in radically different ways, depending on the values and interests of the narrator. Telling about complex and troubling events *should* vary because the past is a selective reconstruction. Individuals exclude experiences that undermine the current identities they wish to claim (remember the Anita Hill-Clarence Thomas hearings).

Of course, some individuals lie (I believe Anita Hill) and investigators may apply narrative methods to try to expose lying and uncover what "really happened." But, as Bruner argued (1987), verification criteria turn slippery: Is it adequate that the "story 'covers' the events of a life? But what is coverage? Are not omissions also important? . . . A rousing tale of a life is not necessarily a 'right' account" (p. 14). Plots are not innocent; they have agendas hidden in them that shape what gets excluded and included, as fact and fiction merge. But

> the stories that persons live by are rarely, if ever, "radically constructed"—it is not a matter of them being made-up, "out of the blue," so to speak. Our culturally available and appropriate stories about personhood and about relationships have been historically constructed and negotiated in communities of persons, and within the context of social structures and institutions. (M. White, 1992, p. 124)

Narratives are laced with social discourses and power relations, which do not remain constant over time (e.g., the category of sexual harassment). There is no reason to assume that an individual's narrative will, or should be, entirely consistent from one setting to the next. "Each telling presents one possible version of the action in question. . . . [T]he idea of narration [invokes] the inevitability of alternative descriptions" (Schafer, 1992, p. xvi). In cases of severe trauma, for example, survivors experience significant gaps in memory and stories change as missing pieces are recovered (Herman, 1992). In a word, traditional notions of reliability simply do not apply to narrative studies, and validity must be radically reconceptualized (see Mishler, 1990).

Validation, the process through which we make claims for the trustworthiness of our interpretations, is the critical issue. "Trustworthiness" not "truth" is a key semantic difference: The latter assumes an objective reality, whereas the former moves the process into the social world. There are at least four ways of approaching validation in narrative work. Each has possibilities but also problems.

PERSUASIVENESS

First, there is the criterion of persuasiveness and its cousin, plausibility. Is the interpretation reasonable and convincing? We have all had the experience of reading a piece of research and thinking "but of course," even when the explanation is counterintuitive (my experience reading Ginsburg's [1989a] *Contested Lives*). Persuasiveness is greatest when theoretical claims are supported with evidence from informants' accounts and when alternative interpretations of the data are considered. The criterion forces us to document interpretive statements for the benefit of skeptical outsiders.

As Van Maanen (1988) showed so cleverly, however, different rhetorical styles can be equally persuasive. (He is curiously silent about validity.) Success depends on "the analyst's capacity to invite, compel, stimulate or delight the audience . . . not on criteria of veracity" (Gergen, 1985, p. 272). Persuasiveness ultimately rests on the rhetoric of writing—on literary practices—and reader response. What may be the most persuasive interpretation of a narrative text at one historical moment may not be later. Our texts have unstable meanings.

CORRESPONDENCE

Second, an investigator can take results back to those studied. Lincoln and Guba (1985) described procedures for "member checks: data, analytic categories, interpretations, and conclusions are tested with those . . . groups from whom the data were originally collected" (p. 314). If the investigator's reconstructions are recognizable as adequate representations, Lincoln and Guba maintain that credibility is increased. In anthropology, informants are beginning to be considered as coauthors (see Behar, 1993) and "the ethnographer as scribe and archivist as well as interpreting observer" (Clifford, 1986, p. 17).

It is desirable, as a general rule, to take work back to the individuals and groups who participated in the study. Bell did this with the DES daughters she interviewed, occasionally giving full transcriptions, while finalizing publication to check that any quoted material had been adequately disguised and securing the informant's consent to use a particular narrative (also see Roberts, 1992). It is important that we find out what participants think of our work, and their responses can often be a source of theoretical insight. Returning our interpretations to their home communities is also politically important. When the activists in Fargo, ND, saw Ginsburg's (1989a) analysis of their abortion struggle, it generated dialogue between women who previously thought they had nothing in common. The afterlife of a study can be as instructive as the formal research itself (Blackman, 1992).

Whether the validity of an investigator's interpretations can be affirmed by member checks is, however, questionable. Human stories are not static, meanings of experiences shift as consciousness changes. Nor can our theorizing across a number of narratives be evaluated by individual narrators.

They may not even agree with our interpretations (so it is important, whenever possible, to clearly distinguish between our views of subjects' lives and their own; see Stivers, 1993). In the final analysis, the work is ours. We have to take responsibility for its truths.

COHERENCE

Third, there is the coherence criterion. Agar and Hobbs (1982) posited three kinds: global, local, and themal. To show that an interpretation is more than ad hoc, coherence must be as "thick" as possible, ideally relating to all three levels. Global coherence refers to the overall goals a narrator is trying to accomplish by speaking. This could mean, for example, that an interviewee wants to tell a story about past actions. Or the goal could be strategic—impression management—as I argue in the divorce study (Riessman, 1990a): A narrator's (global) goal in developing an account (speaking) is to justify an action (divorce). Local coherence is what a narrator is trying to effect in the narrative itself, such as the use of linguistic devices to relate events to one another. To return to the divorce narratives, individuals used contrasts, juxtaposing events and actions, to make their points (e.g., an utterance about how an interaction is "supposed" to take place in marriage was paired with one that described just the opposite). Themal coherence involves content: Chunks of interview text about particular themes figure importantly and repeatedly. To use the divorce example once again, individuals developed their narratives around a set of common themes (e.g., lack of intimacy and companionship) and within an interview a theme was worked over, again and again.

Agar and Hobbs (1982) showed, based on an interview with a heroin addict, how sometimes the three types of coherence offer different perspectives on the same discourse problem, whereas at other times they reinforce the same perspective. But, "if an utterance is shown to be understandable in terms of the three kinds of coherence, the interpretation is strengthened" (p. 29).

Investigators must continuously modify initial hypotheses about speakers' beliefs and goals (global coherence) in light of the structure of particular narratives (local coherence) and recurrent themes that unify the text (themal coherence). Interpretation of meaning is constrained by the text in important ways, offering a check on ad hoc theorizing. It is difficult to apply Agar and Hobbs's framework to interaction in interviews, and the model assumes a rational speaker with a discourse plan, which will not suit all investigations.

PRAGMATIC USE

Lastly, there is the extent to which a particular study becomes the basis for others' work. In contrast to other validation criteria, this one is future oriented, collective, and assumes the socially constructed nature of science. Mishler (1990) argued that "knowledge is validated within a community of scientists as they come to share nonproblematic and useful ways of thinking about and solving problems" (p. 422). Given the conservative nature of normal science (Kuhn, 1962/1970), it is not easy to

> rely on the concepts, methods, and inferences of a study, or tradition of inquiry, as the basis for our own theorizing and empirical work. If our overall assessment of a study's trustworthiness is high enough for us to act on it, we are granting the findings a sufficient degree of validity to invest our own time and energy, and to put at risk our reputations as competent investigators. (Mishler, 1990, p. 419)

However compelling a way of thinking about the problem, Mishler's solution does not help an individual investigator argue in a research report for the validity of a narrative analysis. But we can provide information that will make it possible for others to determine the trustworthiness of our work by (a) describing how the interpretations were produced, (b) making visible what we did, (c) specifying how we accomplished successive transformations (see Figure 1.1), and (d) making primary data available to other researchers. Returning to the examples in Chapter 2, Bell (1988) made the full transcriptions of narratives available upon request; I provided a full text alongside the representation in stanzas and parts. We can, in addition, bring our "foundational assumptions [and values] to the surface, not concealing them underneath the methodological artifice of science" (Agger, 1991, p. 120).

NO CANON

From this brief review, it is apparent that validation in narrative studies cannot be reduced to a set of formal rules or standardized technical procedures (they are insufficient in quantitative research too; see Messick, 1987). Scholars from a variety of social science disciplines make the same point:

The sciences have been enchanted by the myth that the assiduous application of rigorous method will yield sound fact—as if empirical methodology were some form of meat grinder from which truth could be turned out like so many sausages. (Gergen, 1985, p. 273)

The stories we tell, like the questions we ask, are all finally about value. (Cronon, 1992, p. 1376)

Ethnographic truths are . . . inherently partial—committed and incomplete. (Clifford, 1986, p. 7)

There is no canonical approach in interpretive work, no recipes and formulas, and different validation procedures may be better suited to some research problems than to others. For example, it might be useful to determine whether a case study is recognizable to an informant (correspondence), even if the agenda of narrator and analyst are distinct and not always compatible. Plausibility and coherence might be appropriate criteria for comparative case studies. More general theories, developed from narratives, would depend on usefulness to others (pragmatic criteria). Validation in interpretive work is an ongoing, difficult issue that requires attention by narratologists. (For additional ways to think about the topic in qualitative work, see Cronon, 1992; Katz, 1983; Kirk & Miller, 1986; Lather, 1986; Lincoln & Guba, 1985; Packer & Addison, 1989).

Uses and Limitations of Narrative Analysis

The approach I have outlined in this book is appropriate for oral, first-person accounts of experience that take a particular form, what Labov and Waletzky (1967) call "natural narrative." Considerable adaptation and/or other methods will be required if data consist of written narratives, such as letters, archival oral histories, autobiographies, researchers' accounts, scientific representations, and theory itself.

Narrative analysis is not useful for studies of large numbers of nameless, faceless subjects. The methods are slow and painstaking. They require attention to subtlety: nuances of speech, organization of a response, local contexts of production, social discourses that shape what is said, and what cannot be spoken. Not suitable for investigators who seek an easy and unobstructed view of subjects' lives, the analytic detail may seem excessive to those who view language as a transparent medium. As outlined at the beginning of the book, developments in social theory call

70

for complex treatments of language, including its constitutive aspects. A danger is that narrative analysis can reify linguistic structures, however.

There is tension in narrative studies between generalization, on the one hand, and the "unpacking" of speech and close attention to narrative form, on the other. Our ultimate goals as social scientists are to learn about substance, make theoretical claims through method, and learn about the general from the particular. Individual action and biography must be the starting point of analysis, not the end. Ironically, Ginsburg (1989a) can generalize across cases. It is more difficult for others working with personal narratives to make substantive points across interviews. More than one case study is essential if we want to show variation. To reach theoretical levels of abstraction, comparative work is desirable. Yet sample sizes in narrative studies are small, and cases are often drawn from unrepresentative pools. Although a limitation, eloquent and enduring theories have been developed on the basis of close observation of a few individuals (e.g., Breuer's Anna O., Garfinkel's Agnus, Piaget's children). There is a long tradition in science of building inferences from cases.

Narrative methods can be combined with other forms of qualitative analysis, even with quantitative analysis, as argued earlier. This is not an easy task, however. Some fancy epistemological footwork is required because the interpretive perspective that undergirds narrative is very different than the realist assumptions of many forms of qualitative analysis and certainly of quantification. Combining methods forces investigators to confront troublesome philosophical issues and to educate readers about them. Science cannot be spoken in a singular universal voice. Any methodological standpoint is, by definition, partial, incomplete, and historically contingent. Diversity of representations is needed. Narrative analysis is one approach, not a panacea, suitable for some research situations but not others. It is a useful addition to the stock pot of social science methods, bringing critical flavors to the fore that otherwise get lost. Narrative analysis allows for systematic study of personal experience and meaning: how events have been constructed by active subjects.

Note

25. Spence (1982, p. 30-33) makes the distinction in psychoanalysis between historical and narrative truth.

REFERENCES

Agar, M., & Hobbs, J. R. (1982). Interpreting discourse: Coherence and the analysis of ethnographic interviews. *Discourse Processes, 5,* 1-32.

Agger, B. (1991). Critical theory, poststructuralism, postmodernism: Their sociological relevance. *Annual Review of Sociology, 17,* 105-131.

Anderson, K., & Jack, D. C. (1991). Learning to listen: Interview techniques and analyses. In S. B. Gluck & D. Patai (Eds.), *Women's words: The feminist practice of oral history* (pp. 11-26). New York: Routledge.

Arendt, H. (1958). *The human condition.* Chicago: University of Chicago Press.

Atkinson, P. (1990). *The ethnographic imagination: Textual constructions of reality.* New York: Routledge.

Attanucci, J. (1991). Changing subjects: Growing up and growing older. *Journal of Moral Education, 20,* 317-328.

Bakhtin, M. (1981). *The dialogic imagination.* Austin, TX: University of Texas Press.

Barthes, R. (1974). *Introduction to the structural analysis of the narrative* (R. Miller, Trans). New York: Hill and Wang.

Behar, R. (1993). *Translated woman: Crossing the border with Esperanza's story.* Boston: Beacon.

Bell, S. E. (1988). Becoming a political woman: The reconstruction and interpretation of experience through stories. In A. D. Todd & S. Fisher (Eds.), *Gender and discourse: The power of talk* (pp. 97-123). Norwood, NJ: Ablex.

Bell, S. E. (1991). Commentary on "Perspectives on embodiment: The uses of narrativity in ethnographic writing." *Journal of Narrative and Life History, 1*(3), 245-254.

Bennett, T. (1989). From defense to offense. *Women's Review of Books, 7*(3), 14-15.

Berger, P. L., & Luckmann, T. (1966). *The social construction of reality: A treatise in the sociology of knowledge.* New York: Doubleday.

Bertaux, D., & Kohli, M. (1984). The life story approach: A continental view. *Annual Review of Sociology, 10,* 215-237.

Blackman, M. B. (1992). The afterlife of the life history. *Journal of Narrative and Life History, 2*(1), 1-9.

Boje, D. M. (1991). The storytelling organization: A study of story performance in an office-supply firm. *Administrative Science Quarterly, 36,* 106-126.

Brown, L. M., Tappan, M. B., Gilligan, C., Miller, B. A., & Argyris, D. E. (1989). Reading for self and moral voice: A method of interpreting narratives of real-life moral conflict and choice. In M. J. Packer & R. B. Addison (Eds.), *Entering the circle: Hermeneutic investigation in psychology* (pp. 141-164). Albany: State University of New York Press.

Bruner, J. (1986). *Actual minds, possible words.* Cambridge, MA: Harvard University Press.

Bruner, J. (1987). Life as narrative. *Social Research, 54*(1), 11-32.

Bruner, J. (1990). *Acts of meaning.* Cambridge, MA: Harvard University Press.

Burke, K. (1945). Introduction: The five key terms of dramatism. In K. Burke, *A grammar of motives* (pp. xv-xxiii). New York: Prentice-Hall.

Burke, K. (1950). *A rhetoric of motives.* New York: Prentice-Hall.

Bury, M. (1982). Chronic illness as biographical disruption. *Sociology of Health and Illness*, *4*(2), 167-182.

Chafe, W. L. (Ed.). (1980). *The pear stories: Cognitive, cultural and linguistic aspects of narrative production*. Norwood, NJ: Ablex.

Charon, R. (1986). To render the lives of patients. *Literature and Medicine*, *5*, 58-74.

Charon, R. (1989). Doctor-patient/reader-writer: Learning to find the text. *Soundings*, *72*, 1101-1116.

Chase, S. E., & Bell, C. S. (in press). Interpreting the complexity of women's subjectivity. In K. Rogers & E. McMahan (Eds.), *Interactive oral interviewing*. Hillsdale, NJ: Lawrence Erlbaum.

Clark, J. A., & Mishler, E. G. (1992). Attending to patients' stories: Reframing the clinical task. *Sociology of Health and Illness*, *14*(3), 344-372.

Clifford, J. (1986). Partial truths. In J. Clifford & G. E. Marcus (Eds.), *Writing culture: The poetics and politics of ethnography* (pp. 1-26). Berkeley: University of California Press.

Clifford, J. (1988). *The predicament of culture: Twentieth-century ethnography, literature, and art*. Cambridge, MA: Harvard University Press.

Clifford, J., & Marcus, G. E. (Eds.). (1986). *Writing culture: The poetics and politics of ethnography*. Berkeley: University of California Press.

Cohler, B. J. (1982). Personal narrative and life course. *Life-span Development and Behavior*, *4*, 205-241.

Cronon, W. (1992). A place for stories: Nature, history, and narrative. *Journal of American History*, *78*(4), 1347-1376.

Culler, J. (1980). Fabula and sjuzhet in the analysis of narrative: Some American discussions. *Poetics Today*, *1*, 27-37.

Denzin, N. (1988). *Interpretive interactionism*. Newbury Park, CA: Sage.

DeVault, M. L. (1990). Talking and listening from women's standpoint: Feminist strategies for interviewing and analysis. *Social Problems*, *37*(1), 96-116.

Eagleton, T. (1983). *Literary theory: An introduction*. Minneapolis: University of Minnesota Press.

Ellis, C., & Flaherty, M. G. (Eds.). (1992). *Investigating subjectivity: Research on lived experience*. Newbury Park, CA: Sage.

Essed, P. (1988). Understanding verbal accounts of racism: Politics and heuristics of reality constructions. *Text*, *8*(1-2), 5-40.

Fish, S. (1980). Introduction, or how I stopped worrying and learned to love interpretation. In S. Fish, *Is there a text in this class?* (pp. 1-40). Cambridge, MA: Harvard University Press.

Fonow, M. M., & Cook, J. A. (Eds.). (1991). *Beyond methodology: Feminist scholarship as lived research*. Bloomington: Indiana University Press.

Gee, J. P. (1985). The narrativization of experience in the oral style. *Journal of Education*, *167*(1), 9-35.

Gee, J. P. (1986). Units in the production of narrative discourse. *Discourse Processes*, *9*, 391-422.

Gee, J. P. (1991). A linguistic approach to narrative. *Journal of Narrative and Life History*, *1*(1), 15-39.

Geertz, C. (1973). *The interpretation of cultures*. New York: Basic Books.

Geertz, C. (1983). Blurred genres: The refiguration of social thought. In C. Geertz, *Local knowledge: Further essays in interpretive anthropology* (pp. 19-35). New York: Basic Books.

73

Geiger, S.N.G. (1986). Women's life histories: Method and content. *Signs: Journal of Women in Culture and Society, 11*(2), 334-351.

Gergen, K. J. (1985). The social constructionist movement in modern psychology. *American Psychologist, 40*(3), 266-275.

Gilligan, C. (1982). *In a different voice: Psychological theory and women's development.* Cambridge, MA: Harvard University Press.

Ginsburg, F. D. (1989a). *Contested lives: The abortion debate in an American community.* Berkeley: University of California Press.

Ginsburg, F. (1989b). Dissonance and harmony: The symbolic function of abortion in activists' life stories. In Personal Narratives Group (Ed.), *Interpreting women's lives: Feminist theory and personal narratives* (pp. 59-84). Indianapolis: Indiana University Press.

Gluck, S. B., & Patai, D. (Eds.). (1991). *Women's words: The feminist practice of oral history.* New York: Routledge.

Godzich, W. (1989). The time machine. In W. Godzich & J. Schulte-Sase (Eds.), *Theory and history of literature: Vol. 64. Narrative on communication* (pp. ix-xvii). Minneapolis: University of Minnesota Press.

Goffman, E. (1959). *The presentation of self in everyday life.* New York: Doubleday.

Goffman, E. (1974). *Frame analysis.* New York: Harper & Row.

Goode, W. J. (1956). *Women in divorce.* New York: Free Press.

Goodman, N. (1980). Twisted tales, or, story, study, and symphony. In W.J.T. Mitchell (Ed.), *On narrative* (pp. 99-116). Chicago: University of Chicago Press.

Gorelick, S. (1991). Contradictions of feminist methodology. *Gender & Society, 5,* 459-477.

Greenley, A. (1992). *Social theory, social research, and storytelling.* Special session organized and presided by A. Greenley at the annual American Sociological Association Convention, Pittsburgh, PA.

Gusfield, J. R. (1989, February). Sociology and the humanities closing the gap. *Footnotes,* pp. 1, 10.

Halliday, M.A.K. (1973). *Explorations in the functions of language.* London: Edward Arnold.

Heidegger, M. (1927/1962). *Being and time* (J. Macquarrie & E. Robinson, Trans.). New York: Harper & Row.

Herman, J. L. (1992). *Trauma and recovery.* New York: Basic Books.

Hollway, W. (1989). *Subjectivity and method in psychology: Gender, meaning, and science.* London: Sage.

hooks, b. (1989). *Talking back: Thinking feminist, thinking black.* Boston: South End Press.

Husserl, E. (1973). *Experience and judgement: Investigation in a genealogy of logic* (J. S. Churchill & K. Amerikas, Trans.). Evanston, IL: Northwestern University Press. (Original work published 1939)

Hydén, M. (1992). *Woman battering as marital act: The construction of a violent marriage.* Unpublished doctoral dissertation, Stockholm University, Department of Social Work, Stockholm, Sweden.

Jack, D. C. (1991). *Silencing the self: Women and depression.* Cambridge, MA: Harvard University Press.

Jameson, F. (1972). *The prison-house of language.* Princeton, NJ: Princeton University Press.

Jefferson, G. (1979). Sequential aspects of storytelling in conversation. In J. Schenkein (Ed.), *Studies in the organization of conversational interaction* (pp. 219-248). New York: Academic Press.

74

Katz, J. (1983). A theory of qualitative methodology: The social system of analytic fieldwork. In R. M. Emerson (Ed.), *Contemporary field research: A collection of readings* (pp. 127-148). Boston: Little, Brown.

Kirk, J., & Miller, M. L. (1986). *Reliability and validity in qualitative research* (Qualitative Research Methods Series, Vol. 1). Beverly Hills, CA: Sage.

Kleinman, A. (1988). *The illness narratives: Suffering, healing, and the human condition.* New York: Basic Books.

Kuhn, T. S. (1970). *The structure of scientific revolutions* (2nd ed.). Chicago: University of Chicago Press. (Original work published 1962)

Labov, W. (Ed.). (1972). The transformation of experience in narrative syntax. In W. Labov (Ed.), *Language in the inner city: Studies in the Black English vernacular* (pp. 354-396). Philadelphia: University of Pennsylvania Press.

Labov, W. (1982). Speech actions and reactions in personal narrative. In D. Tannen (Ed.), *Analyzing discourse: Text and talk* (pp. 219-247). Washington, DC: Georgetown University Press.

Labov, W., & Waletzky, J. (1967). Narrative analysis: Oral versions of personal experience. In J. Helm (Ed.), *Essays on the verbal and visual arts* (pp. 12-44). Seattle: University of Washington Press.

Laird, J. (1988). Women and stories: restorying women's self-constructions. In M. McGoldrick, C. Anderson, & F. Walsh (Eds.), *Women in families: A framework for family therapy* (pp. 427-450). New York: Norton.

Laird J. (in press). Changing women's narratives: Taking back the discourse. In L. Davis (Ed.), *Building on women's strengths: A social work agenda for the 21st century.* New York: Haworth.

Landau, M. (1984). Human evolution as narrative. *American Scientist, 72,* 262-268.

Langellier, K. M. (1989). Personal narratives: Perspectives on theory and research. *Text and Performance Quarterly, 9*(4), 243-276.

Lather, P. (1986). Issues of validity in openly ideological research: Between a rock and a soft place. *Interchange, 17*(4), 63-84.

Legal storytelling [Special issue]. (1980). *Michigan Law Review, 87*(8).

Lincoln, Y. S., & Guba, E. G. (1985). *Naturalistic inquiry.* Beverly Hills, CA: Sage.

Lynch, M., & Woolgar, S. (Eds.). (1990). *Representation in scientific practice.* Cambridge, MA: MIT Press.

Manning, P. K. (1987). *Semiotics and fieldwork* (Qualitative Research Methods, Vol. 7). Beverly Hills, CA: Sage.

Martin, W. (1986). *Recent theories of narrative.* Ithaca, NY: Cornell University Press.

McAdams, D. P., & Ochberg, R. L. (Eds.). (1988). Psychobiography and life narratives [Special issue]. *Journal of Personality, 56*(1).

McCabe, A. (1991). Haiku as a discourse regulation device. *Language and Society, 20*(4), 577-599.

McCabe, A. (in press). *Chameleon readers.* New York: McGraw-Hill.

McCabe, A., & Peterson, C. (Eds.). (1991). *Developing narrative structure.* Hillsdale, NJ: Lawrence Erlbaum.

Merleau-Ponty, M. (1989). *Phenomenology of perception* (C. Smith, Trans.). London: Routledge. (Original work published 1962)

Merton, R. K., Fiske, M., & Kendall, P. (1990). *The focused interview: A manual of problems and procedures.* New York: Free Press. (Original work published 1956)

Messick, S. (1987). *Validity*. Princeton, NJ: Educational Testing Service.

Michaels, S. (1981). "Sharing time": Children's narrative styles and differential access to literacy. *Language and Society, 10*, 423-442.

Millett, K. (1971). *The prostitution papers: A candid dialogue*. New York: Avon.

Mishler, E. G. (1984). *The discourse of medicine: Dialectics of medical interviews*. Norwood, NJ: Ablex.

Mishler, E. G. (1986a). *Research interviewing: Context and narrative*. Cambridge, MA: Harvard University Press.

Mishler, E. G. (1986b). The analysis of interview-narratives. In T. R. Sarbin (Ed.), *Narrative psychology: The storied nature of human conduct* (pp. 233-255). New York: Praeger.

Mishler, E. G. (1990). Validation in inquiry-guided research: The role of exemplars in narrative studies. *Harvard Educational Review, 60*(4), 415-442.

Mishler, E. G. (1991a). Once upon a time. *Journal of Narrative and Life History, 1*(2), 101-108.

Mishler, E. G. (1991b). Representing discourse: The rhetoric of transcription. *Journal of Narrative and Life History, 1*(4), 255-280.

Mishler, E. G. (1992, August). *Narrative accounts in clinical and research interviews*. Paper presented at conference on Discourse and the Professions, Swedish Association for Applied Linguistics, Uppsala University, Sweden.

Mishler, E. G., Clark, J. A., Ingelfinger, J., & Simon, M. P. (1989). The language of attentive patient care: A comparison of two medical interviews. *Journal of General Internal Medicine, 4*, 325-335.

Mitchell, W.J.T. (1990). Representation. In F. Lentricchia & T. McLaughlin (Eds.), *Critical terms for literary study* (pp. 11-22). Chicago: University of Chicago Press.

Nagel, T. (1986). *The view from nowhere*. New York: Oxford University Press.

Nelson, K. (1989). *Narratives from the crib*. Cambridge, MA: Harvard University Press.

Ochs, E. (1979). Transcription as theory. In E. Ochs & B. B. Schieffelin (Eds.), *Developmental pragmatics* (pp. 43-72). New York: Academic Press.

Packer, M. J., & Addison, R. B. (Eds.). (1989). *Entering the circle: Hermeneutic investigation in psychology*. Albany: State University of New York.

Paget, M. A. (1983). Experience and knowledge. *Human Studies, 6*, 67-90.

Peacock, J. (1992). Afterlives. *Journal of Narrative and Life History, 2*(1), 75-79.

Peller, G. (1987). Reason and the mob: The politics of representation. *Tikkun, 2*(3), 28-95.

Personal Narratives Group. (1989a). Truths. In Personal Narratives Group (Eds.), *Interpreting women's lives: Feminist theory and personal narratives* (pp. 261-264). Indianapolis: Indiana University Press.

Personal Narratives Group (Eds.). (1989b). *Interpreting women's lives: Feminist theory and personal narratives*. Indianapolis: Indiana University Press.

Polanyi, L. (1985). *Telling the American story: A structural and cultural analysis of conversational storytelling*. Norwood, NJ: Ablex.

Polkinghorne, D. E. (1988). *Narrative knowing and the human sciences*. Albany: State University of New York Press.

Rabinow, P., & Sullivan, W. M. (1987). *Interpretive social science: A second look*. Berkeley: University of California Press. (Original work published 1979)

Reinharz, S. (1992). *Feminist methods in social research*. New York: Oxford University Press.

Richardson, L. (1990). *Writing strategies: Reaching diverse audiences* (Qualitative Research Methods Series, Vol. 21). Newbury Park, CA: Sage.

Richardson, L. (1992). The consequences of poetic representation: Writing the other, rewriting the self. In C. Ellis & M. G. Flaherty (Eds.), *Investigating subjectivity: Research on lived experience* (pp. 125-140). Newbury Park, CA: Sage.

Ricoeur, P. (1981). *Hermeneutics and the human sciences: Essays on language, action and interpretation* (J. B. Thompson, Trans.). Cambridge, MA: Cambridge University Press.

Ricoeur, P. (1984). *Time and narrative*. Chicago: University of Chicago Press.

Riessman, C. K. (1987). When gender is not enough: Women interviewing women. *Gender & Society, 1*(2), 172-207.

Riessman, C. K. (1990a). *Divorce talk: Women and men make sense of personal relationships.* New Brunswick, NJ: Rutgers University Press.

Riessman, C. K. (1990b). Strategic uses of narrative in the presentation of self and illness. *Social Science and Medicine, 30*(11), 1195-1200.

Riessman, C. K. (1991). Beyond reductionism: Narrative genres in divorce accounts. *Journal of Narrative and Life History, 1*(1), 41-68.

Riessman, C. K. (1992). Making sense of marital violence: One woman's narrative. In G. C. Rosenwald & R. L. Ochberg (Eds.), *Storied lives: The cultural politics of self-understanding* (pp. 231-249). New Haven, CT: Yale University Press.

Roberts, H. (1992). Answering back: The role of respondents in women's health research. In H. Roberts (Ed.), *Women's health matters* (pp. 176-192). New York: Routledge, Chapman, and Hall.

Rollins, J. (1985). Introduction. In J. Rollins, *Between women: Domestics and their employers* (pp. 5-17). Philadelphia, PA: Temple University Press.

Rosaldo, R. (1989). *Culture and truth: The remaking of social analysis.* Boston: Beacon.

Rosenwald, G. C., & Ochberg, R. (Eds.). (1992a). *Storied lives: The cultural politics of self-understanding.* New Haven, CT: Yale University Press.

Rosenwald, G. C., & Ochberg, R. L. (1992b). Introduction: Life stories, cultural politics, and self-understanding. In G. C. Rosenwald & R. L. Ochberg (Eds.), *Storied lives: The cultural politics of self-understanding* (pp. 1-18). New Haven, CT: Yale University Press.

Roth, S. (1993). Speaking the unspoken: A work-group consultation to reopen dialogue. In E. Imber-Black (Ed.), *Secrets in families and family therapy* (pp. 268-291). New York: Norton.

Ruzek, S. B. (1979). *The women's health movement.* New York: Praeger.

Said, E. W. (1979). *Orientalism.* New York: Vintage.

Sandelowski, M. (1991). Telling stories: Narrative approaches in qualitative research. *Image: Journal of Nursing Scholarship, 23*(3), 161-166.

Sarbin, T. R. (1986a). The narrative as a root metaphor for psychology. In T. R. Sarbin (Ed.), *Narrative psychology: The storied nature of human conduct* (pp. 3-21). New York: Praeger.

Sarbin, T. R. (Ed.). (1986b). *Narrative psychology: The storied nature of human conduct.* New York: Praeger.

Schafer, R. (1980). Narration in the psychoanalytic dialogue. *Critical Inquiry, 7*(1), 29-54.

Schafer, R. (1992). *Retelling a life: Narration and dialogue in psychoanalysis.* New York: Basic Books.

Scheff, T. J. (1990). *Microsociology: Discourse, emotion, and social structure.* Chicago: University of Chicago Press.

Schutz, A. (1967). *The phenomenology of the social world* (G. Walsh & F. Lehnert, Trans.). New York: Northwestern University Press. (Original work published 1932)

77

Shaw, C. (1938). *The jack-roller: A delinquent boy's own story*. Chicago: University of Chicago Press.

Shuman, A. (1986). *Storytelling rights: The uses of oral and written texts by urban adolescents*. Cambridge, England: Cambridge University Press.

Slavney, P. R., & McHugh, P. R. (1984). Life stories and meaningful connections: Reflections on a clinical method in psychiatry and medicine. *Perspectives in Biology & Medicine, 27*, 279-288.

Smith, D. E. (1987). *The everyday world as problematic: A feminist sociology*. Boston: Northeastern University Press.

Sosnoski, J. S. (1991). A mindless man-driven theory machine: Intellectualists, sexualists, and the institution of criticism. In R. R. Warhol & D. P. Herndl (Eds.), *Feminisms: An anthology of literary theory and criticism* (pp. 40-57). New Brunswick, NJ: Rutgers University Press.

Spence, D. P. (1982). *Narrative truth and historical truth: Meaning and interpretation in psychoanalysis*. New York: Norton.

Stewart, D., & Mickunas, A. (1990). *Exploring phenomenology: A guide to the field and its literature*. Athens: Ohio University Press.

Stivers, C. (1993). Reflections on the role of personal narrative in social science. *Signs: Journal of Women in Culture and Society, 18*(2), 408-425.

Tannen, D. (1990). Ordinary conversation and literary discourse: Coherence and the poetics of repetition. In E. H. Benclix (Ed.), *The uses of linguistics* (pp. 15-32). New York: New York Academy of Sciences.

Toolan, M. J. (1988). *Narrative: A critical linguistic introduction*. New York: Routledge.

Van Maanen, J. (1988). *Tales of the field: On writing ethnography*. Chicago: University of Chicago Press.

Veroff, J., Sutherland, L., Chadiha, L., & Ortega, R. M. (in press). Newlyweds tell their stories: A narrative method for assessing marital experiences. *Journal of Personal and Social Relationships*.

West, C. (1984). *Routine complications: Troubles with talk between doctors and patients*. Bloomington: Indiana University Press.

White, H. (1973). *Metahistory*. Baltimore, MD: John Hopkins University Press.

White, H. (1981). The value of narrativity in the representation of reality. In W.J.T. Mitchell (Ed.), *On narrative* (pp. 1-23). Chicago: University of Chicago Press.

White, H. (1989). The rhetoric of interpretation. In P. Hernadi (Ed.), *The rhetoric of interpretation and the interpretation of rhetoric* (pp. 1-22). Durham, NC: Duke University Press.

White, J. B. (1984). *When words lose their meaning: Constitutions and reconstitutions of language, character, and community*. Chicago: Chicago University Press.

White, M. (1992). Deconstruction and therapy. In D. Epston & M. White (Ed.), *Experience, contradiction, narrative, and imagination* (pp. 109-147). South Australia: Dulwich Centre.

White, M., & Epston, D. (1990). *Narrative means to therapeutic ends*. New York: Norton.

Whyte, W. F. (1943). *Street corner society*. Chicago: University of Chicago Press.

Williams, G. (1984). The genesis of chronic illness: Narrative re-construction. *Sociology of Health and Illness, 6*(2), 175-200.

Williams, P. J. (1991). *The alchemy of race and rights: Diary of a law professor*. Cambridge: Harvard University Press.

78

Witherell, C., & Noddings, N. (Eds.). (1991). *Stories lives tell: Narrative and dialogue in education.* New York: Teachers College.

Wolf, D., & Hicks, D. (1989). The voices within narrative: The development of intertextuality in young children's stories. *Discourse Processes, 12,* 329-351.

Wolf, M. (1992). *A thrice told tale: Feminism, postmodernism and ethnographic responsibility.* Stanford, CA: Stanford University Press.

Yans-McLaughlin, V. (1990). Metaphors of self in history: Subjectivity, oral narrative, and immigration studies. In V. Yans-McLaughlin (Ed.), *Immigration reconsidered: History, sociology, and politics* (pp. 254-289). New York: Oxford University Press.

Young, K. G. (1987). *Taleworlds and storyrealms: The phenomenology of narrative.* Boston: Martinus Nijhoff.

Young, K. (1989). Narrative embodiments: Enclaves of the self in the realm of medicine. In J. Shotter & K. J. Gergen (Ed.), *Texts of identity* (pp. 152-165). London: Sage.

ABOUT THE AUTHOR

CATHERINE KOHLER RIESSMAN is Professor of Sociology and Professor of Social Work at Boston University. Both a social worker and a sociologist, she directs a Ph.D. program that connects disciplines. She is the author of *Divorce Talk* (1990), *Qualitative Studies in Social Work Research* (Sage, in press), and numerous academic articles. Her research and publications examine the relationships between women and health, social class and health service use, and gender and divorce. Recent work explores the emergent field of narrative studies. She has taught sociology of the family, medical sociology, family theory, research methods, and qualitative analysis. Riessman is embarking on a study of infertility, supported by the Council for International Exchange of Scholars, the first phase of which will involve participant observation and interviewing of infertile women in India (Kerala State). She is active in the Group for the Advancement of Doctoral Education in Social Work (GADE) and the American Sociological Association, of which she serves on the Medical Sociology Section Council.

Qualitative Research Methods

Series Editor
JOHN VAN MAANEN
Massachusetts Institute of Technology

Associate Editors:
Peter K. Manning, *Northeastern University*
& Marc L. Miller, *University of Washington*

Other volumes in this series listed on outside back cover